SMELLING A RAT & ECSTASY

MIKE LEIGH

Mike Leigh, dramatist, theatre, television and film director, was born in 1943 at Salford in Lancashire. He trained at the Royal Academy of Dramatic Art, at Camberwell and Central Art Schools, and at the London Film School. After this he gained wide acting, directing and designing experience at various theatres, including a season with the Royal Shakespeare Company. His first original play, *The Box Play*, evolved from improvisation at the Midland Arts Centre in Birmingham in 1965. He has continued to use this unique method of creating a script from extensive extemporised rehearsals with great success.

His BBC films include *Hard Labour* (1973), *Nuts In May* (1975), *The Kiss of Death* (1976), *Who's Who* (1978), *Grown-Ups* (1980), *Home Sweet Home* (1982) and *Four Days In July* (1984). His films for Channel-4 are *Meantime* (1983), *The Short & Curlies* (1987) and the feature film *High Hopes* (1988). His earlier feature *Bleak Moments* (1971) was developed from a play of the same name at the Open Space Theatre, London and his many other stage-plays include *Wholesome Glory* (Royal Court, 1973) and *Babies Grow Old* (RSC, 1974).

Abigail's Party (1977) was first produced at the Hampstead Theatre and was later screened as a BBC Play For Today. His other Hampstead plays have been *Ecstasy* (1979), *Goose-Pimples* (1981) which won the Evening Standard Best Comedy of the Year Award, and *Smelling A Rat* (1988). His latest play, *Greek Tragedy*, opened at the Belvoir Street Theatre, Sydney, Australia in 1989.

He is married to Alison Steadman and they live in London with their two sons.

by the same author

Abigail's Party *and* Goose-Pimples

in the same series

Howard Brenton and Tariq Ali	*Iranian Nights*
Caryl Churchill	*Cloud Nine*
	Icecream
	Traps
	Light Shining in Buckinghamshire
Martin Crimp	*Dealing with Clair*
Alexander Gelman	*A Man with Connections* (translated by Stephen Mulrine)
Henrik Ibsen	*An Enemy of the People* (adapted by Arthur Miller)
Terrence McNally	*Frankie and Johnny in the Clair de Lune*
Joshua Sobol	*Ghetto* (English version by David Lan)
Michael Wall	*Amongst Barbarians*
Nicholas Wright	*Mrs Klein*

MIKE LEIGH

SMELLING A RAT

& ECSTASY

N
H
B

NICK HERN BOOKS

A division of Walker Books Limited

A Nick Hern Book

Smelling A Rat & Ecstasy first published in 1989 as an original paperback by Nick Hern Books, a division of Walker Books Limited, 87 Vauxhall Walk, London SE11 5HJ

Smelling A Rat & Ecstasy copyright © 1989 by Mike Leigh

Front cover illustration by Eve Stewart, reproduced with permission

Set by Book Ens, Saffron Walden, Essex
Printed by Billings of Worcester

British Library Cataloguing in Publication Data
Leigh, Mike
   Smelling a rat and Ecstasy
   I. Title   II. Leigh, Mike Ecstasy
   822'.914

   ISBN 1-85459-041-3

SMELLING A RAT

Characters

REX
VIC
CHARMAINE
ROCK
MELANIE-JANE

The action takes place in Rex's bedroom on the day after Boxing Day.

ACT ONE   Late at night

ACT TWO   A few moments later

Time – the present

Smelling A Rat was first performed at the Hampstead Theatre, London on 6 December 1988 with the following cast:

REX	Eric Allan
VIC	Timothy Spall
CHARMAINE	Brid Brennan
ROCK	Greg Cruttwell
MELANIE-JANE	Saskia Reeves

Directed by Mike Leigh
Designed by Eve Stewart
Lighting by Kevin Sleep
Sound by John Leonard

ACT ONE

REX *and Mrs Weasel's bedroom in their flat, which is on the fourth floor of an expensive penthouse-style modern block.*

Built-in wardrobes, into which are recessed a king-size bed and a dressing-table. Pink, gold, silk and bows abound everywhere, but the dressing-table is cluttered and untidy.

On the bed, a carefully-arranged group of at least a dozen assorted soft 'cuddly' toys, including a Kermit the Frog, a Roland Rat, and several rodents, including a large mouse.

Door to main living area beyond, in which are visible a shelf-unit containing various ornaments and other artefacts, including a Spanish bull and some sporting trophies; also visible, part of the stereo system and some tapes and records. The rest of the flat unseen.

Above a bedside-table, a small fire-extinguisher is attached to the alcove; on this bedside-table a large torch, a telephone, a digital alarm-clock. On the other side, a radio/cassette-player, a 'Teasmade', some pill bottles.

Television set and two Spanish dolls on a chest of drawers; a blanket chest; an exercise-bike; an electric golf-putting practiser, with several of its balls lying around it on the floor; a sheepskin rug.

An adjacent en suite *bathroom with sliding, frosted-glass door, and carpeted wall-to-wall, as is the whole room.*

Before Lights Up, i.e. for the Pre-Set, the room is empty, and the door is closed. Darkness, broken only by the suggestion of moonlight through a Venetian blind.

Lights Up. Bright, theatrical music, evoking French farce.

The door opens immediately. REX *puts on the light and enters, briskly, with a duty-free carrier-bag and an airline shoulder-bag; he puts these on the bed. He picks up the torch, turns it on, and quickly inspects the floor of each wardrobe (for mouse-droppings), closing the door after each inspection. He turns off the torch, replaces it, and takes off his raincoat, which he hangs in the wardrobe situated between the door and the bed, closing the wardrobe door. He is wearing loud golfing-clothes, including a cap, which he keeps on throughout the play.*

His luggage can be seen through the doorway; this consists of a suitcase and a bag of golf-clubs; he now brings the latter into the room, checks it over, and places it carefully and lovingly in the same wardrobe.

He gets the suitcase, puts it on the blanket-chest, opens it, and takes out a silk dressing-gown and a toilet-bag; he goes to the bathroom, opens the door, puts on the light, goes in, deposits the gown and the bag, turns out the light, comes out, and closes the door.

Then he efficiently unpacks his shirts, underwear, pyjamas, woollens, handkerchiefs etc. into the chest of drawers, systematically filling one drawer at a time, one after the other. Then he places the suitcase in an overhead cupboard.

By now, the comic music should have finished.

He takes from the airline bag a hip-flask, which he puts on the bed. He puts the airline bag in the wardrobe, and takes the duty-free bag out of the room. He puts out the light in the other room. He comes back into the bedroom and puts on the bedside wall-light. He turns off the main light. He sits on the bed. He takes a swig from the hip-flask, heaves an end-of-hard-day sigh, and puts the flask on the bedside-table.

He picks up a soft toy, looks at it aggressively, and throws it on the floor in the centre of the room. He repeats this with the whole lot, giving some more attention than others, and some none at all, until the bed is clear, and the floor is strewn with cuddly bodies.

He has finished up in a kneeling position on the bed, in order to reach the furthest toys. He stops dead. Muffled talking is heard, off. He springs to the door stealthily, opens it ajar, and listens for a moment. Voices. Somebody turns on the light in the room beyond. He closes the door, and turns off the wall-light.

Pause. Then he gets into the golf-clubs wardrobe, and closes the door. He gets out, takes an airgun out of the bedside drawer, and gets back into the wardrobe, closing the door again.

Only now do we start to register clearly what we can hear, but for practical purposes here is everything that goes on offstage, starting as REX *is disposing of the last of the toys.*

CHARMAINE (*off*). I'll just wait 'ere, Vic.

VIC (*off*). Nah – come on . . .

CHARMAINE (*off*). No!

VIC (*off*). Come on!

Pause.

CHARMAINE (*off*). Is there a switch?

VIC (*off*). Can't see nothing.

CHARMAINE (*off*). There must be one.

VIC (*off*). Oh, 'ere it is – got it! (*Switches light on.*) That's it – bit of light on the subject. Shut the door, then!

CHARMAINE (*off*). You shut it.

VIC (*off*). Arr, there's nothing to worry about!

CHARMAINE (*off*). You 'ave to be careful.

VIC (*off*). There's another switch 'ere. (*Switches another light on.*) Cor', look a' this . . .

CHARMAINE (*off*). I'll just wait 'ere, Vic.

VIC (*off*). Nah, come on.

CHARMAINE (*off*). No.

By this time, REX *is in the wardrobe with the gun.*

VIC (*off*). It's alright for some, init? Money goes to money!

CHARMAINE (*off*). What's it like?

VIC (*off*). Bleedin' 'uge.

CHARMAINE (*off*). Oh! Init lovely?!

VIC (*off*). Well, it don't look like nothing's out of order.

CHARMAINE (*off*). It looks like 'Dynasty'!

VIC (*off*). Inasmuch as these windows ain't been tampered with.

CHARMAINE (*off*). The kitchen's small, in compromise to the lounge.

VIC (*off*). There's another room 'ere. (*He opens the bedroom door, and shines the torch at the exercise-bike*). Oh, look, Charmaine: Weasel's got a gym in 'is flat, the old fart!

CHARMAINE (*entering, she is eating something*). Don't shout, Vic.

VIC. Inasmuch as 'e's got to keep fit for 'is golfin' and sportin' activities.

CHARMAINE. I thought something was wrong.

VIC *shines the torch on the bed.*

VIC. 'E's got a bed in 'ere, an' all.

CHARMAINE. It's 'is bedroom.

VIC. Oh yeah, course it is. (*He shines the torch on the toys.*) What's all that gubbins all over the floor?

CHARMAINE. It's toys, init? 'As 'e got kids?

VIC. Yeah, 'e's got a son.

CHARMAINE. Oh, yeah.

VIC. 'Ang on, 'e's grown up.

CHARMAINE. Well 'e must 'ave grandchildren.

VIC. I don't think 'is boy's old enough to 'ave nippers. (*Pause.*) What're you eatin'?

CHARMAINE. Nothing!

VIC (*shining torch at her*). Yes, you are!

CHARMAINE. 'T's only a bit o' cookin' chocolate.

VIC. What, you nicked it?

CHARMAINE. Well, they'll never know.

VIC. It's all over your face.

CHARMAINE. Is it?!

VIC. Yeah. – No it ain't!

They both laugh, as they will many times throughout the play.
CHARMAINE*'s laugh is a crescendo of a giggle, good-humoured and generous, and not the least bit silly.* VIC*'s laugh might be said to resemble a bark ('*da!*'), but again it has a warmth. It isn't wicked or malevolent.*

CHARMAINE. Turn the light on, Vic – where's the switch?

VIC. There it is.

CHARMAINE. Oh, yeah.

VIC *turns on the light.*

CHARMAINE *gasps.*

VIC. Cor! Plush. (*Pause.*) Well, it don't look like it's been done over.

CHARMAINE. No.

VIC. Inasmuch the blagger nowadays, 'e ain't content with 'alf-inching yer personals, 'e's got to slice up yer furniture with a Stanley knife, and smear shit all over yer walls.

They both laugh.

CHARMAINE. There's Roland Rat!

VIC (*uninterested*). Yeah.

CHARMAINE. They're all the same, in't they, Vic?

VIC. They are.

CHARMAINE. Fancy going away and leaving your place like this.

VIC. 'E probably left in a 'urry.

CHARMAINE. When's 'e coming back?

VIC. End o' the week, I think.

CHARMAINE. Got a lot of wardrobes.

VIC. Yeah. Oh look, Charmaine.

CHARMAINE. What?

VIC. Look at that!

CHARMAINE. What's that?

VIC. 'E's got one of them carpet golf things.

CHARMAINE. Oh, I thought that was a dustpan.

VIC. Don't touch it, it might be a rat-trap!

They both laugh.

VIC. What you do, right? You get a ball (*Demonstrating.*) you knock it in, it shoots out, you knock it in, it shoots out, you knock it in, it shoots out, you knock it in, it shoots out, you knock it in, it shoots out, you knock it in, it shoots out, you knock it in, it shoots out, you knock it in, it shoots out, you knock it in, it shoots out, you knock it in, it shoots out, you knock it in, it shoots out – I saw it on telly – 'ere, don't stand on 'is balls!

They both laugh. VIC *belches.*

VIC. Oh!

CHARMAINE (*amused*). Oh, 'scuse my pig, 'e's a friend!

VIC. Beg pardon, it's the garlic's comin' back up on me.

CHARMAINE. I'd love a bedroom like this.

VIC. Mind you, it was alright, that turkey rosetti, inasmuch as not likin' it don't apply.

CHARMAINE. I 'ad five 'elpings.

VIC. You never!

CHARMAINE. I did.

VIC. You greedy guts!

CHARMAINE. That's why I stayed in the kitchen: I was blowin' off that much.

They both laugh.

VIC. I like the taste of garlic, but I'm not too keen on the smell; but when it 'its the gastric juices, it comes up in the chest, and you've got to get it up out of the old chimney before it flies out of the back door.

They both laugh.

CHARMAINE. 'Ere, can you smell it on me?

VIC (*smelling*). Nah.

CHARMAINE (*smelling*). I can smell something funny on you.

He smells her; he gives her a subtle kiss; they both laugh.

CHARMAINE. Oh, there's them Spanish dolls!

She goes over to inspect them.

VIC. Yeah: flamingo dancers.

CHARMAINE. Got these great big busts, in they?

VIC. She got any drawers on?

They both laugh.

CHARMAINE. Michelle don't even like garlic.

VIC. Don't she? What'd she put it in for?

CHARMAINE. She was always the one 'oo 'ated spicy foods.

VIC. Did she?

CHARMAINE. Mum says it's Mark's fault.

VIC. Well, Mark's a man of the world, in'e, inasmuch as bubble-and-squeak don't suffice.

CHARMAINE. Look at this bed, Vic: init fabulous?

VIC. Yeah, bleedin' gynormous.

CHARMAINE. 'Ere: what d'you think they wanna big bed like this for?

VIC. It's made to 'er specification, init?

CHARMAINE. What d'you mean?

VIC. So she can 'ave an orgy, inasmuch a gang-bang, while 'e's out and about.

They both laugh. Pause. They stand, looking at the bed.

VIC. 'Ere – shall we give it a try?

CHARMAINE *much amused.*

VIC. Go on – get your coat off!

CHARMAINE *amused.*

VIC (*feeling the bed*). Ooh, it's nice an' 'ard.

CHARMAINE *amused.*

VIC (*sitting*). Ooh, solid as a rock!

CHARMAINE. Get off that bed, Vic!

VIC. Come and sit next to me!

CHARMAINE. You'll leave a big bum-print on it.

They both laugh.

VIC. If I 'ad a place like this, I wouldn't want to go on 'oliday, would you, darlin'?

CHARMAINE. No, I wouldn't.

VIC. Mind you, we're talking about a bloke with a disposable income, inasmuch as 'is pockets is so stuffed up, the grass is greener on the other side inasmuch as 'e's never satisfied.

CHARMAINE. Yeah, well 'e's earned it, though, Vic, en' 'e?

VIC. 'E earns it, I'm not saying 'e don't. Inasmuch as 'e charges 'ere, there an' everywhere like a dog with a banger up 'is arse.

CHARMAINE *laughs.*

VIC. But the question is, 'ow does 'e earn it? Inasmuch as it's immoral earnings.

CHARMAINE. What, are you sayin' 'e's a crook?

VIC. 'E's not a crook, 'e's not a crook as such, inasmuch as 'e don't commit burglary, buggery or butchery; but 'e is inasmuch as 'is morals is all up Shit Creek without a paddle.

CHARMAINE *(sitting).* Yeah; you know when you introduced me to 'im at the firm's 'do' that time?

VIC. Yeah.

CHARMAINE. 'E was very charming an' all that, treated me like I was special; but I thought, slimey!

VIC. You thought right. 'E is slimey . . . inasmuch as 'e nods, smiles, licks their arse and takes their money.

CHARMAINE. 'E's two-faced, in' 'e?

VIC. 'E's like a fork-tongued chameleon. It's a different kettle of fish when I was at the Council, inasmuch the public sector; we was providing a service for the eradication of infestations of vermin of ordinary working citizens.

CHARMAINE. Yeah.

VIC. Inasmuch as it was a vocation more than a chore. Inasmuch as we cared.

CHARMAINE. That's right.

VIC. But with Weasel, inasmuch the private sector, the boot's on the other shoe. 'E's a perpetrator, not an exterminator. Inasmuch as 'e manipulates the public paranoia of the population by stickin' 'is finger in the tub of entomophobic parapsychosis, and givin' it a stir.

CHARMAINE. What's that?

VIC. What's what?

CHARMAINE. That tub o' stuff.

VIC (*looking round*). What tub o' stuff?

CHARMAINE. 'E sticks 'is finger in?

Pause.

VIC. No! Entomophobic parapsychosis!

CHARMAINE. Yeah – what is it?

VIC. The fear of all crawling insects in every man, woman and child.

CHARMAINE. Oh. (*Pause.*) You're not sorry, are you?

VIC. Sorry about what?

CHARMAINE. About leavin' the Council.

VIC. Well, I am inasmuch as I'm a cog in the wheel of Capitalism. Mind you, the extra money comes in 'andy, dunnit?

CHARMAINE. You're telling me. And the free car.

VIC. Yeah. But I've got to put up with it, inasmuch as kowtowing to all 'is foibles and deceits.

CHARMAINE. What d'you mean?

VIC. Take last Tuesday.

CHARMAINE. What?

VIC. 'E bleeps me, I ring 'im back, I say, "Ello Rex, 'ow are you?" 'E says, 'Never mind that – I've got a woman with a spider problem, inasmuch as they're drivin' 'er potty.' I said, 'Rex, spiders is a non-target species, inasmuch as they're of no public health significance; unlike mus musculus, the common 'ouse-mouse, and our old friend rattus rattus.' 'E said, 'Don't give me all that, if she wants to think spiders is a problem, let 'er think spiders is a problem, and it ain't for the likes of you to put 'er on the straight-and-narrow about it, thanking you very much! Get round there, give 'er a good spraying, and eradicate 'em off the face of 'er living-room.' I said, 'I can't do that, Rex: it's against my Code of Ethics.' 'E said, 'Don't you argue the toss with me, do as you're told! Get on your bike, get round there, knock 'em on the 'ead, and charge 'er accordingly.' All 'e cares about is money. 'E's money-mad!

CHARMAINE. I don't blame 'im. I 'ate spiders.

VIC. There's nothing wrong with spiders. Spiders is on our side. You don't see no flies when there's a spider about – they got more sense, they keep out of the way! Spiders is the pest-controllers of the insect world. Ain't no flies on spiders. Inasmuch the fly, 'e's a disgusting bugger. 'E sits on shit (CHARMAINE *starts laughing*), shits on it, eats it, flies on your egg-and-bacon, shits on that, spreads disease and pestilence all over it, then you eat it.

CHARMAINE's mirth has taken her to a lying-down position.

VIC. Oh, look: there's a spider crawling up your leg there.

CHARMAINE (*sitting up*). Where, Vic?!

VIC. There . . .

CHARMAINE shrieks and giggles as VIC runs his finger up her leg . . . this develops into a gentle, jokey cuddle on the bed. Suddenly, CHARMAINE gets up.

CHARMAINE. Vic!

VIC. What's up?

CHARMAINE. Someone might 'ear us.

VIC. 'Oo?

CHARMAINE. Upstairs . . .

VIC. Don't worry about that – these places are built like 'Itler's bleedin' bunker, inasmuch the Reichstag.

CHARMAINE. They wasn't the same thing, Vic.

VIC. Oh, yeah.

CHARMAINE. They might call the police.

VIC. Don't worry about the Old Bill – they're too busy spoiling people's Christmases.

CHARMAINE. Vic – get off that bed! Look at the state of it!!

She starts straightening the bedding.

VIC. What? 'T's alright – just pull it over!

CHARMAINE. You pull it over!

VIC. Don't fret yourself.

CHARMAINE. 'Ey, Vic.

VIC. What?

CHARMAINE. Does 'e know about you?

VIC. 'Oo?

CHARMAINE. Weasel.

VIC. Know about what?

CHARMAINE. About when you was a kid.

VIC. No, course not! I weren't gonna tell 'im, was I? Wouldn't a got the job. Any'ow, it never came up. Bloke like 'im wouldn't understand. None of 'is business! 'T's all way back in the past, don't count no more. Nobody knows about it. Any'ow, I've 'ad the job for three years now, so it don't apply.

CHARMAINE. Them coppers come round knew about it.

VIC. That's different; they checked the Central Computer, 'cos we was under suspicion.

CHARMAINE. You was under suspicion – I'd been cleared.

VIC. Yeah, well that's the bastard system for you, ain't it, eh? Once they get you on the list, you stay on the list. Don't matter if it's something you did when you was fourteen.

CHARMAINE. Yeah, but you never done it, though, did you?

VIC. But it was me what was sent away, though, wonnit – Muggins?

CHARMAINE. I know, Vic.

VIC. Stays as a black mark against you for the rest of your life. Inasmuch as it's a stigma; I've been stigmatised.

CHARMAINE. Well, I'm sure 'e's got a skeleton in 'is cupboard!

Pause.

VIC. Let's 'ave a look, shall we?

They both laugh. VIC *shines his torch for a few moments at some of the wardrobes; then he creeps up to one, 'Grand Guignol' style, and opens it, mock-surreptitiously.* CHARMAINE, *who has been giggling throughout this, creeps up behind him, and –*

CHARMAINE. Woo!

VIC (*genuinely surprised*). Aaargh!! (*Slams door.*)

CHARMAINE *is convulsed with mirth.*

VIC. Frightened the bleedin' life out of me!

Both laugh; their laughter subsides. CHARMAINE *sits on the dressing-table stool.*

CHARMAINE. Oo, I'm tired, Vic.

VIC *crosses to sit on the blanket-chest.*

VIC. Yeah . . . me an' all.

Pause.

CHARMAINE. Mum's been putting the pressure on Michelle.

VIC. What for?

CHARMAINE. About 'aving a baby.

VIC. Bduh! 'T's bleedin' typical, init?

CHARMAINE. I think Michelle's got her flat too nice, really.

Pause.

VIC. 'Ere: 'oo's to say you ain't gonna be first?

CHARMAINE. I 'ope I will be first, Vic!

VIC. Yeah!

CHARMAINE. I'm getting on.

VIC. Oh, poor old soul!

They both laugh.

VIC. Any'ow, Mark fires blanks, dun 'e?

CHARMAINE. Well, you needn't be so cocky!

They both laugh.

Pause.

VIC. Well . . . we've done our duty; might as well bugger off.

CHARMAINE. Yeah. (*Pause.*) 'Ey, Vic: look at the state of her dressing-table!

VIC. What?

CHARMAINE. Untidy, in't she?

VIC. She's a slut inasmuch as she's untidy in 'er 'abits.

CHARMAINE. Is she?

VIC. It's a well-known fact, inasmuch as she's a bit flighty.

CHARMAINE. 'Oo told you that?

VIC. Leveritt.

CHARMAINE. What'd 'e say?

VIC. 'E told me she was a piss-artist and a slag. Mind you, you can take what 'e says with a pinch of salt, inasmuch as 'e's got something 'orrible to say about everything. 'E wouldn't give you the pickings of 'is nose!

CHARMAINE *laughs.*

VIC. Mind you, with all that shit, and this flotsam and jetsam, the proof of the pudding's in the eating, init?

CHARMAINE *offers him a dish of false finger-nails.*

CHARMAINE. 'Ere – d'you want one?

VIC. What's that? (*He takes one.*) Aaargh! Get out of it!! Load of old finger-nails!

CHARMAINE (*amused*). They're only false ones!

VIC. 'Orrible!

CHARMAINE. Vic, I shouldn't 'ave done that!

VIC. You talking about?

CHARMAINE. I've put my fingerprint on it now.

VIC. Don't be daft!

CHARMAINE. 'Ave to clean it off.

VIC. Ain't doin' nothin' criminal.

CHARMAINE (*taking a tissue*). I'll use one o' these.

VIC. We're doing a favour for someone!

CHARMAINE. That's better.

VIC. Oh, look: 'e's got one o' them 'on-suet' bathrooms.

He opens the bathroom door.

CHARMAINE (*looking in the mirror*). Got chocolate on my teeth, Vic.

VIC turns on the bathroom light.

VIC. Cor' – look a' that!

He goes in. CHARMAINE follows as far as the bathroom doorway.

CHARMAINE. You're not going to use the library now, are you?

VIC. I'd rather 'ave a shit on me own pot, any day. Oh, look – 'e's got a bidette!

CHARMAINE *has gone in.*

CHARMAINE. Yeh, well 'e needs it, don' 'e?

VIC. She does, you mean.

They both laugh.

VIC. You know what that's for, don't you?

CHARMAINE. Yeah, I know what it's for, Vic.

VIC. Washing your bits out. (*Coming out of the bathroom.*) You get a jet of 'ot water right up your kibosh.

They both laugh.

CHARMAINE (*coming out*). 'E's left 'is toilet-bag be'ind.

VIC. I told you, 'e left in a 'urry. 'T's alright 'avin' one o' them, init, though, eh? Straight out o' bed, on the bog, off the bog, back into bed again! No roaming about in the dark, dark, dank corridor, stubbing your toe an' effin' and blindin'!

CHARMAINE *laughs.*

CHARMAINE. Turn the light off, Vic. Shut the door.

But he was already doing both things in any case.

CHARMAINE. It's a good thing you're wearing them driving-gloves.

VIC. I keep telling you – there's nothing to worry about, inasmuch as it's a good deed well done.

CHARMAINE *is half-way out of the bedroom.*

VIC. Oh look, Charmaine!

CHARMAINE *(coming back)*. What?

VIC. Look at that!

CHARMAINE. What's that?

VIC. That thing on the wall. Fire-extinguisher.

CHARMAINE. You gave me a shock, Vic!

VIC. You know what that's for, don't yer?

CHARMAINE. What?

VIC. Smoking in bed.

    CHARMAINE *laughs.*

VIC *(doing voice)*. 'Oh; oh, oh, darlin', pass me the fire-extinguisher – I'm on fire!'

CHARMAINE. Vic!

VIC. What?

CHARMAINE. You shouldn't say that!

    VIC *laughs.*

CHARMAINE. 'Ere – what's she got?

VIC. Load of old pills, inasmuch she must be a junkie, an' all.

    They both laugh.

CHARMAINE. Right, Mr Nosey: what's this, then?

VIC. Pot calling the kettle black, init?

CHARMAINE. What is it?

VIC. That's a 'ip-flask.

CHARMAINE. Yeah.

VIC. 'Ere, that's for 'er midnight guzzling.

CHARMAINE. That's right.

VIC. D'you know, I got a call-out once, from this big 'ouse in Golders Green, and there was a woman there 'oo was so alcoholic, she used to 'ave a bottle of cooking-sherry in 'er bedside cabinet. So she could 'ave a swig in the middle o' the night.

CHARMAINE. 'Ow d'you know that?

They are leaving the room.

VIC. 'Er maid told me when she gave me a cuppa tea – 'orrible, it was, tasted like perfume!

He turns off the bedroom light. CHARMAINE *is looking at the shelf-unit. He joins her.*

VIC. Cor'. Look at that lot!

CHARMAINE. Yeah.

VIC. 'T's like a bingo display, init?

CHARMAINE. 'T's not 'omely, is it, Vic?

VIC. Nah; cold.

He turns to another corner of the room.

VIC. Oh, 'ere's all 'is guns! I've used them!

CHARMAINE. What for?

VIC. Pigeon and squirrel killing.

CHARMAINE. Ah!

They disappear towards the front door.

VIC (*off*). You wouldn't want them in your cornflakes, would you? It's all part of the job.

CHARMAINE (*off*). 'Ey, Vic: d'you think I could use the toilet?

VIC (*off*). Yeah – course you can.

CHARMAINE *comes back into the bedroom without putting on the light.*

CHARMAINE. Well I ain't goina do nothing in it.

VIC. What d'you wanna use it for, then?

CHARMAINE *laughs.*

VIC (*off*). I'll 'ave a sit-down.

CHARMAINE (*going to the door*). No, Vic – you come in 'ere with me!

VIC (*off*). Oh, leave off!

CHARMAINE. Come on, Vic: I won't be a minute.

VIC (*off*). Bleedin' 'ell!

He comes in.

CHARMAINE. Better take my coat off.

She does so. VIC *sits on the bed.*

CHARMAINE. Open the door, Vic.

VIC gets up, goes to the bathroom door, and opens it.

CHARMAINE. Turn the light on.

He does so. She goes in.

CHARMAINE. Shut the door, Vic.

He does so.

CHARMAINE (*off*). Put yer fingers in yer ears.

VIC. I've 'eard you tinkling 'undreds o' times!

They both laugh.

VIC (*belching*). Oh! (*Another belch.*) Oh! (*Another belch.*) Ah! I'm all stuffed up.

CHARMAINE (*off*). I shouldn't 'ave 'eld on so long.

VIC. I reckon it's the most I've eaten any Christmas all my life. I ain't stopped, 'ave we?

CHARMAINE (*off*). Well, I am definitely going on a diet after this.

VIC. Mind you, that's what it's all about these days, init, Christmas? Stuff it down, stuff it down, stuff it down as much as you can . . . 'T's all about sluff and glotteny. Ain't about the worship and the celebration of the birth of Jesus Christ. Not that I give a gypsy's toss about all that . . . inasmuch as I think it's a load of mumbo-jumbo. Inasmuch as I think it's a load of old bullshit. Mind you . . . the living standards is much 'igher than what it used to be. Notwithstanding 'arf the world's fat, and 'arf the world's dying of starvation. And the other 'arf doesn't know its arse from its elbow. Specially at Christmas- time. There's no rime or reason to it. Plenty o' poor lost souls spending Christmas in a cardboard box, with nothing but a burning piece of plank for a bit o' warmth; nothing but a plastic cup o' soup doled out the back of a van by a patronising God-botherer with nothing better to do on a Christmas night inasmuch as, 'That's yer lot for yer Christmas fare and sustenance!' Mind you; when I was a kid, you was lucky to get so much as an orange and a clip round the ear'ole for Christmas.

CHARMAINE (*off*). I can't wait to get these shoes off – my feet's killing me.

VIC. I did get a kaleidoscope one year. It was bleedin' useless 'cos it was smashed up one end, and all the bits 'ad fallen out. Christmas Day was the only day my ole man didn't knock us about. And that was only in the mornin'! (*Pause.*) What're you doin', 'avin' a bath?

CHARMAINE (*off*). No, but I need one – I smell 'orrible.

VIC. Go on – 'ave one.

They both laugh.

VIC *shines his torch on several of the wardrobe doors, making light patterns with the beam. He gets up, goes over to one of the wardrobes, opens it, and has a peep inside. Then he gets in, and closes the door.*

By now the toilet has flushed, and CHARMAINE *has washed her hands. Pause.*

CHARMAINE (*at the door*). Open the door, Vic. (*Pause.*) Vic. (*Pause.*) Vic. (*Pause.*) Vic, open the door!!! VIC!!!

She opens the door herself, and comes out, heading for the other room.

CHARMAINE. Vic!

VIC (*in wardrobe*). Grrrr!!

CHARMAINE. Stop it, Vic!

VIC (*in wardrobe*). Grrrrrr!!

CHARMAINE *picks up her coat.*

CHARMAINE. Vic, stop it!!!! I'm leaving, Vic – I'm goin' now.

VIC *bursts out of the wardrobe with a mock-ferocious growl. They both collapse all over the room with uncontrollable mirth.*

CHARMAINE. } Ssh! Ssh! Ssh!

VIC. } Ssh! Ssh!

Their mirth subsides. They embrace in the middle of the room.

VIC. Ah! Ah! Did I frighten it?

Pause. They listen. Voices off.

VIC. D'you 'ear that?

CHARMAINE. Is it next door?

VIC. Sounds like someone's comin' in!

CHARMAINE. D'you think it's burglars?

VIC. Yeah – might be. 'Ide in there! (*He means the wardrobe he's just been in.*)

CHARMAINE. I'm not goin' in there!

VIC. Go on – I'll stand by the door and whack 'em on the 'ead when they come in.

CHARMAINE. Don't be stupid, Vic – you get in with me!

VIC. I'd better 'ad, they might be violent.

CHARMAINE gets in the wardrobe, still holding her coat. VIC tries to get in with her.

VIC. I can't get in there – there's no room! I'll get in the next one.

He does so, but gets out again, and rushes to the bathroom to put out the light.

CHARMAINE (*coming out*). Where are you going, Vic?

VIC. I'm turning the light off, shut up! Get in!!

He runs back and gets into his wardrobe again, closing the door. A feather boa is caught outside the door. He pulls this discreetly in.

At this point we again start to register more precisely what we can actually hear. But for practical purposes, here is all that happens offstage, starting just before VIC says, 'Ah! Ah! Did I frighten it?'

ROCK and MELANIE-JANE are outside the door of the flat.

MELANIE-JANE (*off*). My grandma lives in a block of flats. She does. But she only lives on the third floor, so you don't have to use the lift if you don't want to. Is this your front door?

ROCK (*off*). Yeah.

MELANIE-JANE (*off*). Oh, look – there's another front-door. You've got your own front-door keys, haven't you?

ROCK (*off*). Yeah.

MELANIE-JANE (*off*). It's nice, isn't it? 'Cos then you can decide whether you want to come here, or whether you want to go there – whatever you want!

From about here we hear ROCK *and* MELANIE-JANE *more clearly.*

MELANIE-JANE (*off*). They've left the lights on. They have. It's big, isn't it?Shall I close the door? It's bigger from the inside than it is from the outside. I'll close the door.

She closes the door. ROCK *now appears in the bedroom doorway.*

MELANIE-JANE (*off*). I've closed the door!

ROCK *pauses, and puts on the light. Then he comes in, stops, looks at the toys on the floor and around the room in general, and goes and sits on the bed.*

Throughout this, MELANIE-JANE *has continued regardless . . .*

MELANIE-JANE (*off*). Oh, what's that? I haven't seen one of those before! Is this where you have your dinner parties? I like this flat, it's gorgeous. There's a horrible ugly bull on top of that bookshelf. There is.

She comes into view through the doorway.

I went to a bullfight when I was in Barcelona with my Daddy. It gave me a toothache. What are you doing? You've got some guns. You have. Why have you got these guns? I don't like guns.

Pause. She is in the doorway.

(*Giggling.*) This is a big bedroom, isn't it? Is this your bedroom? (*Pause.*) Is it, Rocky?

Pause.

ROCK. No.

Pause.

MELANIE-JANE. It's your Mummy and Daddy's bedroom, isn't it?

Pause.

ROCK. Yeah.

Pause.

MELANIE-JANE (*giggling*). Oh, dear! Who do those toys belong to?

Pause.

ROCK. They're my Mum's.

MELANIE-JANE. Is that your Daddy's exercise-bike?

ROCK. No, it's my Mum's.

MELANIE-JANE (*giggling*). Are we allowed to be in here? We're not, are we?

Pause.

ROCK. Yeah.

Pause.

MELANIE-JANE. I'm not allowed in my Mummy and Daddy's bedroom. I'm not. Oh, yes I was, on my twenty-first birthday! People were allowed to put their coats on the bed. Well, it wasn't actually on my birthday, it was at my party. 'Cos my birthday was on the Thursday, and my party was on the Saturday. We were going to have my party on the Thursday, but I work late on a Thursday. Well, I did that Thursday, anyway. So we decided to have it on the Saturday, so that people could sleep late on the Sunday. (*Giggles.*) But you know – you were there, weren't you? (*Giggles.*) Did you put your coat on my Mummy and Daddy's bed?

Pause.

ROCK. No.

Pause.

MELANIE-JANE. Where's your bedroom?

Pause.

ROCK. I don't live here, do I?

MELANIE-JANE. No, I know you don't live here now; but what d'you do when you come to visit?

ROCK. There isn't another bedroom. This is the only one.

MELANIE-JANE. Where do you sleep, then?

Pause.

ROCK. My Dad doesn't want me here.

MELANIE-JANE. Doesn't he? (*Giggles.*) That's not very nice, is it? My Daddy likes me living at home. He does. I think he does anyway. I need to go to the toilet . . . Can I use the toilet, please? Where's the bathroom?

Pause.

(*Giggling.*) Where is it?

Pause.

ROCK (*gesturing vaguely*). It's over there.

MELANIE-JANE. Oh, yes. I didn't see it. I should've gone in the pub, but I don't like that toilet very much. (*Looking in.*) You've got a bidet! My Mummy wants a bidet. My Mummy's agoraphobic. Daddy won't let her have one, though. (*Going in.*) Oh, (*Giggling.*) you can see yourself when you're sitting on the toilet! Where's the light switch? – Oh, there it is! (*Turns on the light.*) I won't be a minute. (*Closes the door. Giggling.*) I can see you through the door. I can. Can you see me?

Pause. Opens the door.

ROCK. Yeah.

MELANIE-JANE. Don't you want to go into the living-room? Watch the television? The film? (*Pause. Giggles.*) You'll have to go out. You will. I don't think I can do it if you're sitting there. (*Pause.*) Please, Rocky . . .

Pause. Then she runs over to him, takes him by the hands, and tries to pull him up.

MELANIE-JANE. Come on – don't be a silly sausage! I'll have an accident, and then you'll get into trouble with your Mummy and Daddy. Please, Rocky – don't be a spoilsport. (*He allows her to pull him up.*) That's right, there's a good boy. In here.

(She pushes him into the living-room. Off.) You sit down there, and get comfortable. *(She comes back into the bedroom.)* I won't be long! *(She goes into the bathroom, and closes the door.)*

Pause: nothing happens on stage. Then ROCK *enters, now wearing his earphones. His Walkman is on – loud enough for the heavy beat of the music to be audible. He holds the packet of cooking-chocolate, and is eating some. He walks round the bed, and stands looking at it for a while, near the bathroom door.*

The toilet is flushed. Pause. MELANIE-JANE *opens the door. On seeing* ROCK, *she stops in her tracks. Pause. She turns off the bathroom light. They look at each other. Pause. Then she runs across the room to the door. Pause. She goes out, and immediately re-enters.*

MELANIE-JANE. Aren't we going to sit on the sofa? I think I'll just take my coat off.

She goes out. ROCK *moves as if to come round the bed and follow her, but instead stops and sits on the end of the bed. His tape is still audible.*

MELANIE-JANE *(off)*. Can I have a look at some of your records? *(Pause.)* Liberace! You've got Liberace. *(She appears in the doorway, holding a Liberace album; she has taken off her coat and her glasses.)* He's my Mummy's favourite. *(ROCK turns off the tape, and takes off his cans.)* She used to play him all the time at home; and then he died; and now Daddy doesn't let her play him any more. *(Pause.)* Oh, look at those trophies! *(She goes out to them, remaining in view.)* My Daddy plays golf. He does. I used to wait for him in the car while he practised at this special place; all you could see was the golf-balls flying through the air . . . you couldn't see who was hitting them, though.

ROCK. There's over two million prostitutes in Thailand.

Pause.

MELANIE-JANE. Shall we sit in there?

ROCK. My Dad used to make me carry his golf-clubs.

MELANIE-JANE. My brother used to carry my Daddy's golf-clubs. He got five pounds a week pocket-money for it.

ROCK. Did he? You wouldn't catch my Dad giving me anything. You know when I was working at Pizza-Pronto? I was only earning seventy pounds a week, and he wanted me to give him fifty!

MELANIE-JANE. Did he?

ROCK. Yeah. (*Pause.*) That was when I left college. It wasn't my fault I didn't get my 'A' Levels.

MELANIE-JANE. 'A' Levels are horrible.

ROCK. That would have only left me twenty pounds a week to buy all my clothes with. (*Pause.*) Anyway, he doesn't need the money – he's practically a millionaire. He's a bloody sadist. He locked me out of the house. He got me this bedsit without even telling me – he moved all my stuff in there.

MELANIE-JANE. Did he?

ROCK. Even my stereo. I wasn't going to live there. I had to stay with a mate. I never gave him the money, though. I went back home, and all my stuff was there. He never said anything.

MELANIE-JANE. Didn't he?

ROCK. No. I woke up on the Saturday, though, and there was an estate agent in my bedroom, measuring everything.

MELANIE-JANE (*sitting on the bed, not next to him*). Your Daddy let an estate agent in your bedroom? Did he?

ROCK. He put the house up for sale. He didn't even tell my Mum.

MELANIE-JANE. My Daddy wouldn't let an estate agent in my bedroom. He wouldn't

ROCK. Then he went and bought this place.

Pause.

MELANIE-JANE. This is a hard bed, isn't it?

Long pause.

ROCK. My Dad's a wanker.

Long pause.

MELANIE-JANE. Are you going to stay here tonight? (*Long pause.*) Or are you going back to Chris's? (*Long pause.*) Which?

Pause. MELANIE-JANE *sits next to* ROCK.

Can I have some of your chocolate? Can I? What have you got? It's cooking chocolate! You're eating cooking chocolate. You are. My Daddy might have to go to Sweden on business. He had to 'phone them yesterday. He's been there before, though. He had to go to the office. He was there all afternoon. Fancy having to work on Boxing Day! Mummy wouldn't speak to anybody. I'll just have a little piece. (*She takes some chocolate, and puts the packet on the bed beside her.*) D'you know what I did on Christmas Day? I had to lay the dinner table, and I put the forks where the knives were meant to be, and the knives where the forks were meant to be. (*Giggles.*) Aren't I silly? Daddy hit me on the back of the head . . . with a cork table-mat . . . I've still got the bump; I play with it in bed. D'you want to feel it? (*She offers it to* ROCK; *he doesn't react.*) He was only joking though. (*Pause.*) These table-mats have scenes on them, of Stratford-upon-Avon. They have. And this one has Anne Hathaway's cottage on it, with a little picture in the corner of Lady Macbeth with her daggers. (*Pause.*) Does your Mummy dye her hair?

ROCK *kisses* MELANIE-JANE, *quickly and suddenly. At first, she responds; then she jumps away from him.*

You taste of chocolate! – Oh dear, I'm sitting on it! (*Pause. Then she takes off a shoe.*) My shoes need re-heeling. I don't wear these to work, though, 'cos they're too high. Oh, look – there's Kermit the Frog. (*She joins Kermit on the floor.*) Hello, Kermit the Frog! (*Doing voice.*) 'Hello, Melanie-Jane' (*Giggles.*) I used to have a Kermit the Frog puppet. I did. I used to stick my hand up his bottom to make his mouth move.

Pause.

ROCK. I saw Keith Chegwyn the other day in W. H. Smith's.

MELANIE-JANE. Did you? What was he doing?

Pause.

ROCK. I dunno. Buying something.

MELANIE-JANE. Perhaps he was doing his last-minute Christmas shopping. What's that? Oh, it's a mouse!

ROCK *goes to the dressing-table.*

MELANIE-JANE. I've still got three teddy-bears at home. I have. D'you know what I call them? I call them Teddy-Bear 1,

Teddy-Bear 2 and Teddy-Bear 3. Teddy-Bear 3's my
favourite. I let him sleep with me in my bed. I've got a single
bed. I haven't got a double bed. I've never slept in a double
bed . . . well, not properly . . .

ROCK *has picked up a perfume-spray; he gives it a brief,
unexpressive squirt. Pause.*

What're you doing? (*Pause. He looks at her. Then another squirt!*)
Is that your Mummy's perfume? (*Another squirt.*) Are you
spraying your Mummy's perfume? (*Another squirt. She goes
towards him.*) Don't . . . you'll get it on the carpet. Mm – that's
a nice smell, isn't it? (*He sprays her.*) Don't spray me! (*He sprays
her again; she runs away.*) Don't! (*Returning.*) I want a go! (*Spray.*)
Rocky! Give it to me! (*Spray.*) Help!!! (*She runs away again.*) I'm
going to put my shoe on. You're not allowed to spray me
until I've got my shoe on. Pax! (*Holding up one hand, crossing her
fingers. She stands on one foot in order to put her other shoe on. He
sprays her. She falls over, giggling hysterically.*) That's not fair –
that's cheating! I'm going to get Kermit the Frog to protect
me. (*She picks up Kermit, and holds him out in front of her.*) You've
got to give it to us now. (*He sprays them. She puts Kermit behind
her with his arms around her waist.*) You're not allowed to spray
Kermit! Give it to me! I want it now! You've got to give it to
me! (*Struggling with* ROCK.) Rocky! Let me have it! (*She falls
onto the bed, with a bit of help from* ROCK. *She lies there, giggling.
Pause.*) That's not fair. That's not supposed to happen. (*Getting
up.*) I'll just put it back. Where does it go? Oh, yes. (*She puts
the perfume-bottle back. To Kermit.*) You sit there. (*Sits Kermit on
the stool; as an afterthought she crosses his legs. Pause. She is still
giggling.* ROCK *and* MELANIE-JANE *are standing close to each
other.*) That was a good game, wasn't it? (*He kisses her. Again she
responds at first for a moment, then pushes him off.*) You are funny!
(*She runs across the room.*) I think I'll have a cigarette . . . I'll
just go and get one.

Exit MELANIE-JANE. ROCK *hovers by the bed.*

MELANIE-JANE (*off*). Can I have a cup of tea?

She comes back with a cigarette and a large, expensive table-lighter.

This is nice, isn't it? My Daddy sells these. He sells
computers, as well. (*She lights the cigarette;* ROCK *takes out a
handkerchief, and blows his nose.*) I'll just put it back.

Exit MELANIE-JANE. ROCK *takes off his jacket and moves to the head of the bed on the bathroom side. He takes the cassette out of his Walkman, and puts it in the radio/cassette player by the bed.*

MELANIE-JANE *appears in the doorway. She is wearing her glasses.*

Ooh, dear. I'd better not smoke in here. (*Tries to disperse the smoke.*) We had ham at Christmas as well as turkey, because Grandma Beetles doesn't like turkey; she says it reminds her of Grandpa Beetles. (*Pause. The music – Madonna – has started.*) Does Madonna *know* Michael Jackson . . . d'you think . . . ?

Pause.

ROCK. I dunno.

MELANIE-JANE. I need an ashtray. (*Sees one by the bed.*) Oh. I wish my Mummy and Daddy smoked.

She sits on the bed. They are now both sitting on the bed, one on each side. Pause.

ROCK. Jogging causes depression.

MELANIE-JANE. Does it? Oh, dear!

ROCK. People who jog a lot get jogger's nipple.

MELANIE-JANE. What's jogger's nipple?

Pause.

ROCK. Dunno.

Pause.

MELANIE-JANE. Sounds like an ice-cream. (*Pause.*) Did you try my socks on?

ROCK. No.

MELANIE-JANE. Don't you like them?

ROCK (*no response.*)

MELANIE-JANE. I got all my Christmas presents from work this year. I did. 'Cos you get discount. D'you get discount at your shoe-shop?

Pause.

ROCK. Yeah.

MELANIE-JANE. Did you buy anybody any shoes for Christmas?

ROCK. No.

MELANIE-JANE. No . . . I didn't get anybody any toys. (*Pause.*)
I'm not looking forward to the January sales . . . it's not fair.
Oh, dear! – I'd better not get ash on the bed . . . keep it nice
and clean or your Daddy will be cross.

ROCK. My Dad has the whole flat sprayed each month.

MELANIE-JANE. Does he? What with?

Pause.

ROCK. A spray.

MELANIE-JANE. One of those air-fresheners? We're not allowed
to have those in our house. We're not. 'Cos Mummy's
allergic to them. Daddy says the house smells like a Chinese
brothel on Confucius's birthday. He does – he always says
that! (*Giggles.*)

ROCK. It's insecticide.

Pause.

MELANIE-JANE. What's insecticide?

ROCK. What they spray.

MELANIE-JANE. Ergh! Yukkie!

ROCK. When we lived in Tudor Road, they used to get me out of
bed so they could spray my bedroom.

MELANIE-JANE. Who used to get you out of bed?

ROCK. My Dad. His men used to come round with a spray-gun.
He was always getting them round. He makes them do things
for him.

MELANIE-JANE. What sort of things?

ROCK. They have to put up fences; mend the toilet; drive him
about . . . They even had to pick up my Mum once when she
broke down on the North Circular. She was wearing a bikini.
(*Pause.*) He thinks he's still in the Army.

MELANIE-JANE. My brother was in the Army. He was. The
King's Troop Royal Horse Artillery. He's not any more,
though. He sells computers. He rode his horse at Lord

Mountbatten's funeral. He did. We watched him on the television – it was really funny. He was hoping to be at the Queen Mother's funeral before he left. He was really disappointed. They have special black horses just to pull the coffins . . . (*Pause.*) Do the men have to spray this bed? Do they? There was a spider in my wardrobe last summer; there was; it was Daddy's birthday . . . I bought him a bull-worker . . . he was really cross. It was one of those whitey spiders – well, sort of grey. I opened the door, and it just disappeared! It ran into one of my shoes; I didn't know which one, so I waited for it to come out . . . but it didn't. I stood there for ages. In the end I just closed the door and went downstairs. Everybody was waiting for me. (*Pause.*) Have you ever seen a cockroach?

ROCK (*no response*).

MELANIE-JANE *moves to face* ROCK *directly, at close quarters, kneeling.*

MELANIE-JANE. When I was seven I had all my hair cut off. I did, 'cos I had lice. It wasn't very nice. I couldn't stop scratching for ages. I kept thinking they were going to crawl down my face and get into my head through my mouth, or through my ears, or up my nose . . . and eat my eyeballs from behind, and have my brains for breakfast.

ROCK *embraces and kisses her again; they roll over on the bed; for a few moments* MELANIE-JANE *responds, making furtive clutching movements, scratching* ROCK's *back with small gestures. Then she suddenly withdraws, and sits up abruptly.*

Be careful of my glasses, Rocky! I don't want to break them again. They're very exclusive frames.

MELANIE-JANE *gets up.* ROCK *stays on the bed.* MELANIE-JANE *starts moving around the room. The following should be slightly frenetic.*

D'you think I should get contact lenses? Daddy thinks I should get coloured ones. Mummy doesn't, though; she says my eyes are a nice colour the way they are. I'm going to have a go on this. (*She mounts the exercise-bike, but she doesn't pedal.*) D'you know what the time is? I'll have to be getting a taxi soon. (*She gets off the bike, and goes to the dressing-table.*) We had a nice time this evening, didn't we? Look at my hair. (*Going towards the door.*) Do you have a taxi number? (*Exits.*) I wonder what time it is. (*Enters.*) Have you ever played 'Trivial Pursuits'? OH, LOOK: THERE'S AN ALBATROSS!!! (*Big burst of giggles. She sits on the blanket chest and examines her hair.*) I've got a lot of split ends. (*Opens and closes the blanket chest.*) Oh, it's like a coffin. (*Crosses the room.*) We'll see each other in the week, though, won't we, Rocky? I like the sausages with the herbs in them best. (*Touching the wardrobes containing* VIC *and* CHARMAINE.) Your Mummy and Daddy must have a lot of clothes. (*Moves away from these wardrobes, and opens and closes a nearby one. Pause.*) We've known each other for a long time, haven't we, Rocky? Since when we were at college together. Can I have a little peep? (*She opens and closes yet another wardrobe, then moves back towards* VIC *and* CHARMAINE's *two, stopping at the next one along, which she opens and closes. Pause.*) Do you like me, Rocky?

ROCK. *No response. Long pause.*

> MELANIE-JANE *goes to* CHARMAINE's *wardrobe.*

MELANIE-JANE. I think I'll have a look in this one. (*Tries it.* CHARMAINE *is holding it closed from inside.*) Oh – it's locked!

She opens the next one, and sees VIC. *She slams it shut, screaming; she bolts across the room.*

MELANIE-JANE. THERE'S A MAN IN THAT CUPBOARD!!!!!

> ROCK *stares at her.*

THERE IS!!! (*She is extremely distraught.*)

THERE'S A MAN IN THERE!!!!

She takes a pillow from the bed, and hugs it.

ROCKY!! THERE'S A MAN IN THE CUPBOARD!!!

Crying, agitated, unhinged, terrified.

ROCKY!!!!

Long pause, during which she becomes increasingly upset.

I DON'T LIKE THIS GAME!!!!!

She rushes into the toilet, and locks the door.

Very long pause. MELANIE-JANE's *crying dies down, first to a whimper, and then to silence.* ROCK *is baffled and immobile.*

Eventually VIC's *door opens slowly, and he emerges from the darkness and from Mrs Weasel's gaudy collection, still holding his torch . . .*

VIC. Good evening, Master Weasel . . . inasmuch I presume you're Master Weasel . . . (*He closes the door.*) Er . . . my name is Mr Maggott; inasmuch Victor Maggott . . .

CHARMAINE *opens her door, and begins to emerge. She is still holding her coat.*

VIC. This is my wife, Mrs Maggott . . . she, er . . .

CHARMAINE *holds up her coat, as though to protect herself from seeing the unseeable. She runs across and out of the room;* VIC *follows her . . .*

VIC. Charmaine! Charmaine! (*Stopping in the doorway.*) Everything ain't what it looks like . . . inasmuch what you're seeing . . . ain't what it seems; d'you get what I'm saying? What I'm saying . . . is that I've been requested, as it were. . . to give the place the once-over, inasmuch check it out . . . and make sure that everything is shipshape and Bristol-fashion.

CHARMAINE (*off.*) We never touched nothin'!!!

VIC. No, that's right, we ain't – only door-fastenings and window-casements; and I can safely report that there is no visible sign of breaking-and-entering, inasmuch skulduggery and other various felonies.

CHARMAINE (*appearing*). Anyway, my husband's been wearin' 'is driving gloves.

VIC. That's right: a Christmas present from my good lady wife here. A very practical gift indeed. Only we was led to believe that the flat was empty, inasmuch as your mother and father were on their Christmas vacation inasmuch as there was no-one 'ere.

CHARMAINE. That was what we was told, anyway, wanit, Vic?

VIC. We was on our way 'ome inasmuch as we don't actually live in this vicinity.

CHARMAINE. No, we live in North London.

VIC. Inasmuch the London Borough of Islin'ton.

CHARMAINE. That's right.

VIC. D'you know it, by any chance?

CHARMAINE. No, 'e won't know it, Vic.

VIC. 'E might . . . It's got two prisons.

CHARMAINE. My sister always 'as us down after Christmas.

VIC. We was killing one bird with two stones.

CHARMAINE. We all go round to my Mum's on Christmas Day, don't we, Vic?

VIC. Wouldn't miss it for the world!

CHARMAINE. Her 'usband works for Britannia Airways.

VIC. Check-in.

CHARMAINE. They live just round the corner from 'ere – Thamesmeade Court: d'you know it?

VIC. Nice flats, private.

CHARMAINE. She give us a lovely evening, dint she, Vic?

VIC. She always does us proud.

CHARMAINE. She's very generous, my sister, in't she, Vic?

VIC. Very generous!

CHARMAINE. Anyway, you was just doin' someone a favour, wun' you, Vic?

VIC. That's right!

CHARMAINE. Mr Stoat.

VIC. That's right – Roy Stoat. You know Roy Stoat, don't you? – your father's second-in-command. A decent sort . . .

CHARMAINE. I told you we shouldn't 'ave said yes.

VIC. 'E's only shown me nothing but friendship and kindness, inasmuch as one good deed deserves another!

CHARMAINE. 'E's too good-natured, my 'usband – I'm always telling 'im that!

VIC. Don't be daft, darlin'. (*Pause.*) What it is . . . what it is, you see, inasmuch . . . is that 'e's been obligated; 'e's 'ad to go to Uttoxeter to visit 'is in-laws; but between me, you and the gate-post, inasmuch within these three walls, 'e's doin' a bit o' moonlighting on the Q.T. . . . 'cos 'e's supposed to be on call over the Christmas Season, keeping people's festive tables free from unwanted visitors, notwithstanding a favour pledged to your father to stick 'is mush in this place and give it a quick shufti to alleviate 'is worries and vexations; but what with 'is own domestic ramifications, 'e's asked me to do the favour for 'im . . . ain' 'e?

CHARMAINE. Yeah . . .

VIC. Inasmuch . . . in lieu . . .

CHARMAINE. 'E come round to us with the keys . . . last Wednesday, wunit, Vic?

VIC. That's right.

CHARMAINE. Day before Christmas Eve. And I offered 'im a cup of tea . . .

VIC. It was too early for alcoholic beverages, notwithstanding the time of year.

CHARMAINE. But 'e didn't want one, 'cos 'is wife and kids was downstairs in the car with the luggage . . .

VIC. They was worried about finding the M1.

CHARMAINE. We're five floors up.

VIC. You know Roy Stoat, don't yer?

ROCK (*no response*).

VIC. Big, tall, skinny fellow with a skull face; looks like an American, wears a baseball 'at. Comes from Morden.

CHARMAINE. Talks real quiet . . .

Pause.

VIC. I'd've thought you'd 'ave known 'im.

Pause.

ROCK. I do know 'im.

CHARMAINE. There you are, Vic.

VIC. Well, that's 'im!!!!

Pause.

ROCK. D'you work for my Dad?

CHARMAINE. Yes, 'e does!

VIC. 'Course I do, I've worked for your father for nigh on three years, all but a few months, inasmuch as I've never 'ad a day off!

CHARMAINE. Except for 'is Grandad's funeral.

VIC. Yeah, but that weren't with bad 'ealth!

CHARMAINE. No!

VIC. 'E's my boss. I work for 'im . . . and I'm doin' a favour for 'im but 'e don't know 'e's 'avin' a favour done for . . .

CHARMAINE. Yeah, cos your Dad's in Spain with your Mum, ain' 'e?

Pause.

ROCK. No.

VIC. Ain't 'e?

Pause.

ROCK. No. (*Pause.*) They're not in Spain.

Pause.

VIC. Oh, that's right – 'e's in Tenerife, ain't they?

ROCK. No.

VIC. Ain't they?

ROCK. No.

VIC. Where are they, then?

Pause.

ROCK. They're in Lanzarote.

VIC. Well, it's the same thing, init?

Pause.

ROCK. No.

VIC. Yes, it is.

ROCK. No, it's not.

VIC. 'Course it is! 'T's the Canary Islands, init? Lanzarote, Gran

Canaria, Tenerife! Inasmuch Lanzarote is a volcano, and it rose out of the sea, and all of its sand is volcanic ash and therefore bleedin' useless for making sandcastles.

But ROCK *is inspecting* VIC's *wardrobe.*

ROCK. Yeah, but they're not in Tenerife.

VIC. It's alright – there's nobody else in there.

CHARMAINE. Vic – the keys. You've got the keys!!

VIC. Oh, yeah! Roy give me the keys, didn' 'e? 'Ere y'are: two Yale, one Chubb! 'Ere, why don't you check my pockets while you're about it?

CHARMAINE. You can look in my bag, if you like.

VIC. Yeah, 'ave a look in 'er bag – look, nothing!

CHARMAINE (*looking in her bag*). Well, I do admit I did borrow one of your Mum's tissues.

VIC. It's alright, I can pay for that, I've got money. (*Jingles his pocket.*)

ROCK *is now inspecting* CHARMAINE's *wardrobe.*

CHARMAINE. Everything's just as it was in there.

VIC. She wouldn't touch nothing that weren't 'ers.

CHARMAINE. You can ask my sister – we told 'er we was coming 'ere on the way 'ome, didn't we, Vic?

VIC. That's right!

CHARMAINE. Phone 'er and check, if you like.

VIC. Yeah – go on, give 'er a call!

CHARMAINE. The car, Vic!!

VIC. What?

CHARMAINE. Downstairs!

VIC. Oh yeah, course: me car! You know the firm's cars don't yer? White Ford Fiestas with the name down the side: 'Vermination. The Pest Patrol.'

CHARMAINE. Why don't you come and 'ave a look?

VIC. Yeah – didn't you see it parked downstairs in front of that smashed-up Jag?

CHARMAINE. It's got all 'is stuff in it, enit, Vic?

VIC. That's right, inasmuch all the tools of my trade. You've got yer bait-boxes, you've got yer sticky-boards, you got yer Brodifacoum, yer Villsen Pyramids, you've got yer insecticide – I've even got a brand-new Insectocutor, ready for installation, 'aven't I, Charmaine?

CHARMAINE. Yeah – it's like a walking death-trap in there – I can 'ardly get in.

VIC. Would you care to accompany me to the vehicle, then? Inasmuch see 'oo I am, what I'm talking about? Your wish is our demand, young Mr Weasel.

ROCK has now inspected two more wardrobes, and is on to his fifth; he ignores VIC *and* CHARMAINE.

VIC. I don't know what else to say to convince you . . .

CHARMAINE. I 'ope your girlfriend ain't poorly.

ROCK goes and has a look through the bathroom door.

VIC. Yeah – shock can give you the collywobbles . . .

CHARMAINE. Yeah . . .

VIC. Inasmuch the gyp.

CHARMAINE advances towards ROCK, *who remains with his back to them.*

CHARMAINE. I'm sorry we spoiled things for you.

ROCK (no response).

CHARMAINE. 'Scuse me . . .

Pause. MELANIE-JANE *is moving towards the door.*

CHARMAINE. Oh, I think she's comin' out!

Pause. MELANIE-JANE *opens the door, and comes out, holding the pillow.*

CHARMAINE. Ah, 'ere she is!

VIC. Eh . . . she's as right as ninepence, ain't she?

CHARMAINE. Yeah, she is. 'Ow are you now, love? (*To* ROCK.) You should get 'er a brandy.

> VIC *assumes a bizarre posture.*

VIC. See! I ain't the bogeyman!

> VIC *and* CHARMAINE *laugh hugely.*

CHARMAINE. D'you know, I've been married to him for six years, and I still get a fright when I look at him!

VIC. Shut up! Giz a kiss!!

> VIC *and* CHARMAINE *laugh some more.*

ROCK. Are you gonna tell my Dad?

VIC. What?

ROCK. That you saw us here.

VIC. No, course not! We wouldn't do a thing like that – would we, Charmaine?

MELANIE-JANE. Why, aren't we allowed to be here, then?

ROCK. Yeah.

VIC. It's none of our business, is it? Inasmuch as it's your alienable prerogative to be in this residence, inasmuch as you're a member of the Weasel family, inasmuch as it's your God-given right!

MELANIE-JANE. Are we?

CHARMAINE. Anyway, we was just as scared as you was.

VIC. We thought you was intruders.

CHARMAINE. Yeah, I thought my end had come!

VIC. You was lucky I didn't give you a whack on the nut.

CHARMAINE. And when you was talking about spiders, I could feel them crawling all over me!

> VIC *and* CHARMAINE *laugh uproariously, whilst* ROCK *crosses, and inspects the last remaining wardrobe not containing* REX; VIC *and* CHARMAINE *join him and have a look.*

VIC. Nothing.

CHARMAINE. No.

Long pause, during which CHARMAINE *silently but expressively communicates sympathy to* MELANIE-JANE, *e.g. miming 'Are you alright?', shuddering at shared horrors of spiders and bogeymen in cupboards, raising eyes heavenwards about the men, etc.*

VIC. Well . . . this ain't going to get the pig a new bonnet, is it?

CHARMAINE. No.

VIC. Inasmuch time's getting on, and these two young people want to get to their bed.

VIC *and* CHARMAINE *laugh uproariously.* ROCK *moves towards the last* (REX's) *wardrobe, but –*

VIC. Right, then: if everything's alright with you, we'll be taking our leave, eh, Charmaine?

CHARMAINE. Yeah.

VIC. Would you by any chance 'ave such a thing as a pencil and a piece of paper?

ROCK. There's a message-pad by the fridge.

VIC. Good! 'Cos what I'm going to do for you is, I'm going to log my credentials, inasmuch give you my name, address, telephone number and postal code . . .

CHARMAINE. That's a good idea, Vic.

VIC. And should anything untoward arise from our untimely visitation, do not 'esitate to contact me, inasmuch let me know.

ROCK, VIC *and* CHARMAINE *have filed out of the room, followed after a moment by* MELANIE-JANE, *who now stands alone in the doorway, still holding the pillow.* CHARMAINE *reappears.*

CHARMAINE. It was nice meeting you.

MELANIE-JANE. It was very nice to meet you, as well.

VIC (*off*). Oh, good – a detachable pad.

MELANIE-JANE. Bye bye!

CHARMAINE. 'Bye.

CHARMAINE *returns to the others in the kitchen.* MELANIE-JANE *comes back into the room; she replaces the pillow, sits on the bed, and proceeds to put on her shoes.*

VIC (*off*). Now what I'm gonna do is to write my name and address on 'ere and give it to you . . . and I want you to fold it neatly, and put it in yer inside pocket, and nobody need know about it . . . alright?

MELANIE-JANE has got her shoes on, and is quietly recomposing herself.

VIC (*off*). Right. Now . . . we are Mr . . . and Mrs . . . Victor . . . Maggott . . . and we live at seventy-four –

REX pops his head round the wardrobe door, thinking the room is empty. He is still holding the gun.

MELANIE-JANE (*screaming and running across the room*). NO!!! NO!!!!

REX immediately withdraws into the wardrobe, and closes the door. MELANIE-JANE is further confused and hysterical.

CHARMAINE rushes in, followed by VIC.

CHARMAINE. } What's the matter? Wait a minute!
VIC.   } What's 'appening?

MELANIE-JANE, now very fraught, starts throwing stuffed animals at REX's wardrobe; some of these go in CHARMAINE's direction, possibly hitting her. CHARMAINE and VIC rush out, closing the door. REX comes out of the wardrobe.

REX. Alright, calm down! (*MELANIE-JANE runs towards the bathroom.*) Stand still! – No, don't go in there! (*She goes in.*) I want to go in there – I want to use it!!! (*She has locked the door;* REX *has rushed across to stop her, but he is too late.*) Come out, you stupid girl!!! COME OUT!!!!

VIC has crept back into the room, unseen by REX, at whom he now stands gaping. REX stops, turns round, and stares back at VIC. Pause.

VIC. Fuck my old boots!!!!

Exit VIC, followed by REX.

REX. Maggott!! Maggott!!! MAGGOTT!!!!

Blackout

ACT TWO

The same, a few moments later. ROCK *is outside the bathroom, facing* REX. REX *is very tense. He is pointing the gun at* ROCK.

REX. Talk to 'er! Go on! She's your bloody girlfriend – tell 'er! She's in my bathroom! What are you waiting for? Don't just stand there!

Pause.

Look at you! You pillock! You great streak of yellow piss! You're bloody useless!!

VIC *appears at the door, with* CHARMAINE *behind him.*

VIC. 'Scuse me, boss . . .

REX. What do you want, Maggott?

VIC. Er –

REX. Wh?

VIC. You are 'ere, then?

REX. What?!

VIC. Inasmuch you ain't an apparatition, inasmuch you ain't been beamed down from another planet?

CHARMAINE *giggles.*

VIC. – Shut up, Charmaine – inasmuch as I ain't goin' round the bend and you're 'ere in your flat in your lovely bedroom 'ere?

REX. Yes, I'm here alright, Maggott – large as bloody life!

REX *waves the gun at* VIC, *and goes over to the bathroom.*

VIC. Alright, boss!

Pause.

REX. Right! Maggott: come 'ere!!

VIC. What?

REX. Sit on the bed!

VIC. I beg your pardon?

REX. And your lady wife!

VIC. What, on the bed?

REX. You heard me – come on!

VIC. What for?

REX. 'Cos I say so – COME ON!!!

VIC. Alright, Rex – anything you want. I can explain everything.

REX. Oh, can you?

VIC. Yeah. Come on, darlin'.

    CHARMAINE sits on the bed.

CHARMAINE. D'you 'ave a nice Christmas, Mr Weasel?

REX (*going towards the door*). Bloody awful, thank you!

VIC. Go easy with the blunderbuss there, boss!

REX. Shut up. And don't move.

    He goes and shuts the door. Pause.

CHARMAINE (*getting up*). What's 'e up to?

VIC. I dunno. (*Belches.*)

CHARMAINE. Vic!

VIC. That's shock, that is.

CHARMAINE. Are you alright?

VIC. Yeah. (*Pause.*) Where'd 'e bleedin' pop up from?

CHARMAINE. 'E must 'ave come in through the front door.

VIC. When?

CHARMAINE. When we was in the kitchen.

VIC. No, 'e never.

CHARMAINE (*to ROCK*). Didn't 'e?

VIC (*to ROCK*). Did 'e?

ROCK (*no response*).

VIC. You was facing that way! D'you see 'im?

CHARMAINE. I don't think 'e did, Vic.

VIC. Course not.

CHARMAINE. What's she up to?

VIC. Eh? (*Pause.*) Oi!

CHARMAINE. What?

VIC. 'E was already in 'ere, wan' 'e?

CHARMAINE. Don't be so daft, Vic – where?

VIC. I dunno. (*Inspecting the bed.*) No – it's a divan.

> *Pause.*

CHARMAINE. We'll be lucky to get out of 'ere alive!

VIC. Oh, don't worry about that.

CHARMAINE. Don't tell me not to worry, Vic – I'm scared stiff of that thing!

VIC. 'E's playin' cops-and-robbers – it's only an airgun; it can't kill yer – it'll just give yer a nasty sting up yer bum.

CHARMAINE. I 'ope you're right.

VIC. Course I'm right. That thing's too small.

CHARMAINE. What thing?

VIC. That hottoman. (*He is referring to the blanket chest.*)

CHARMAINE. Yeah, it is. (*Giggles.*)

VIC. There's nowhere else *to* 'ide.

CHARMAINE. Only the cupboards.

VIC. Don't be ridiculous!

> *They both laugh.*

VIC (*to* ROCK). Anyway, you checked 'em all didn't yer?

ROCK (*no response*).

VIC. Did ya?

ROCK (*no response*).

VIC. Sir?

Pause.

CHARMAINE. 'E never done this one, Vic.

VIC. Eh?

Pause. Then CHARMAINE *gasps and springs away from* REX's *wardrobe.* VIC *rises. They gravitate towards each other. Long pause.*

VIC. Shit!!

VIC *and* CHARMAINE *rush to the door.*

CHARMAINE. I can't 'ear nothing.

VIC. No. Very irregular.

CHARMAINE. It is, init?

Pause. ROCK *drifts towards the bathroom.*

VIC. Well, this is a right old two-an'-eight.

CHARMAINE. It's the last time you're doing a favour for anyone.

VIC. Leave off, darlin'.

CHARMAINE. It is, Vic!

VIC. Inasmuch as it was a matter of a friend in need.

CHARMAINE. Some friend! 'E's left us lookin' like a right couple o' monkeys, en' 'e?

VIC. I wish we was monkeys – we could shin down the drainpipe!

CHARMAINE *(giggles. Pause)*. I'm 'ungry, Vic – are you?

VIC. Peckish.

CHARMAINE. Is that place up Mount Pleasant open?

VIC. What, Agamenmon?

CHARMAINE. Yeah.

VIC. Yeah, 'e's open till three o'clock in the morning, seven days a week.

CHARMAINE. Oh, that's right. I fancy a kebab.

VIC. I could sink a shish.

Pause.

CHARMAINE. What're we going to do, Vic?

VIC. Well, all we can do is explain what we was doin' 'ere, and bugger off.

CHARMAINE. 'E knows what we was doin' 'ere.

VIC. 'Ow? Oh, bollocks – course 'e does!

CHARMAINE. 'Ere, Vic . . .

VIC. What?

CHARMAINE. What was that I said about 'im?

VIC. I can't remember.

CHARMAINE. I could cut my tongue out.

VIC. It ain't no use in crying over spilt milk; inasmuch sticks and stones; what's done is done; the truth's out; what goes up can't come down; it ain't a jack-in-the-box. Any'ow, let 'e 'oo chucks the first brick be free of guilt, inasmuch people in glass 'ouses shouldn't throw stones. Two wrongs don't make a right!

CHARMAINE. I know that, Vic!

VIC. When in Rome . . . a dog learns by example.

CHARMAINE. You said 'e was a villain.

VIC. No, I never.

CHARMAINE. You did, Vic.

VIC. Not inasmuch. Any'ow, what about what you said about 'is missis?

CHARMAINE. What did I say about 'is missis?

VIC. You said she was a dipsomaniac.

CHARMAINE. I never said that – you said that!

VIC. No, I never!

CHARMAINE. Yes, you did, Vic. I don't even know what it means.

VIC. Course you do!

CHARMAINE. What?

VIC. It means you can't get enough of it.

CHARMAINE. Enough of what?

VIC. You know – bunk-ups.

CHARMAINE. Vic! That's a nymphomaniac!

VIC. Oh, yeah.

Almost simultaneously, they remember ROCK's *presence. Pause.*

VIC. Oh, that's a nice telly, init?

CHARMAINE. Yeah, it is, init?

VIC. State Of The Art! Has it got a Teletext, inasmuch the
Oracle? I reckon in a 'undred years' time, tellies'll be so
small, you'll be able to clip 'em on your glasses . . . wear 'em
while you're drivin' your car! You'll be able to call it, like a
dog, "Ere, come 'ere, Telly, there's a good boy . . . turn over,
Channel-19, aaah!' You'll be able to cook liver on your
pocket microwave.

CHARMAINE. Yeah, well . . . we're all in a state of shock ain't
we?

VIC. Inasmuch we're all tarred with the same feather!

CHARMAINE. That's right, Vic. I mean, I know 'e's your Dad,
an' you love 'im, right? But 'e is usin' threatening behaviour
against us, in'e, Vic?

VIC. That's right. But a man can do what 'e likes in the privacy of
'is own 'ome, inasmuch an Englishman's 'ome is 'is castle,
even if it's a prefab. But 'e is performin' a bit preposterous,
inasmuch out of order. I bet 'e give you the pip, didn' 'e?
inasmuch the willies ('scuse my French) with all that argein'
an' bargein' an' shoutin' an' bawlin'?

CHARMAINE. Where's your Mum, eh?

VIC. What's your Dad doin', bakin' a cake?

CHARMAINE. I bet you wish she was 'ere, don't you? (*Going to
the bathroom door.*) I wish my Mum was 'ere.

VIC. I know – 'e's been and dumped 'er in Tenerife, in 'e, poor
old cow?

CHARMAINE. Vic!!!

VIC. Oh, beg pardon . . .

CHARMAINE (*through door*). 'Ello, darlin' . . . what you doin'?

VIC. What's she up to, eh?

CHARMAINE. She's got a towel over 'er 'ead.

VIC. She's sitting up in the corner like Little Miss Muffet.

CHARMAINE. She's terrified!

VIC. Yeah, course she is – she's like a rabbit.

CHARMAINE. No, she ain't.

VIC. Yeah, she is.

CHARMAINE. Ow?

    Pause.

VIC. A rabbit . . . a rabbit . . . strolls out of a 'edge in a country
    lane . . . mindin' 'is own business in the pitch black; stands
    in the middle of the road, scratchin' 'is arse, thinkin' about
    the Meanin' of Life. All of a sudden, without warnin', a car,
    doin' a thousand miles an hour, 'urtles towards 'im; does 'e
    'op it? – no, o' course not: 'e stands there, inasmuch
    spiflicated. In a trance. Like a moron. Hypnotised. By its
    'eadlights. Frozen, like a packet of peas. (*Makes death noise.*)
    Dead.

CHARMAINE (*to* MELANIE-JANE). What you up to? Eh?

VIC (*to* ROCK). 'T's 'uman nature, ain't it? (*He bangs on the glass
    door with his torch.*)

CHARMAINE. Vic!!

VIC. She moved!

CHARMAINE. Course she moved!

VIC. Just making sure she ain't paralysed.

    CHARMAINE *tuts.*

VIC. Inasmuch she ain't got lockjaw.

    Enter REX, *the gun in one hand, a glass of whisky-and-ice in the
    other.*

REX. Right. That's one crisis dealt with. Nearly got caught short
    there.

VIC. Are you feeling better in yourself, then, Rex?

REX. Yes, thankyou, Vic.

VIC. Did you nip out there, boss . . . to turn your bike around?

REX. No. There's more than one way to skin a cat.

VIC. Yeah, course. 'Nuff said . . .'

CHARMAINE. It's embarrassing, ain't it, Mr Weasel?

VIC. Course, relieving yourself can put a different colour on things –

CHARMAINE. Yeah.

VIC. – Inasmuch improve your temperament for the better, with all due respects.

REX (*pointing gun at bathroom and Maggotts*). She's still in there.

CHARMAINE *gasps.*

VIC. 'T's alright, darlin'. Sorry we moved, Rex!

REX. What?

CHARMAINE. From the bed, Mr Weasel.

REX (*waving gun*). I want her out!!

VIC. Yeah – course you do!

CHARMAINE. Is this glass shatterproof, Mr Weasel?

REX. I'm not breaking that!

CHARMAINE. Oh, I didn't mean that, I was just –

VIC. Only she's in a bit of a state . . . She's behavin' like . . . a retracted porcupine . . . turned in on itself, and sticking out its egretious prongs . . . inasmuch 'ibernating.

CHARMAINE. I think a cup of tea might bring her round, Mr Weasel.

REX. Oh, you do, do you?

CHARMAINE. Now, I'm not bein' cheeky nor nothing, Mr Weasel, don't get me wrong.

VIC. We was addressin' ourselves to the problem in 'and.

CHARMAINE. That's right, Vic.

VIC. I only 'ope she don't start frothin' at the mouth, get it all over your carpets there; I can see they're not an offcut remnant inasmuch as they're worth more than four pounds fifty a square yard.

REX. No. Has he talked to her yet?

CHARMAINE. No.

VIC. I'm sorry to say young Master Weasel hasn't piped up, squeaked or burped a syllable.

REX. That's not surprising. How am I going to flush her out?

VIC. Well, I reckon you've got a bit of a problem on your 'ands 'ere, Rex; inasmuch as you're dealing with a Homo Sapiens. Now if she was a rodent, inasmuch a recalcitrant rat gone to ground, it would just be a matter of carefully-placed bait-trays, inasmuch Neo-Serexa.

REX. Neo-Serexa! You're supposed to be using the Klerat.

VIC. I'm sorry, boss, but I reckon the Klerat's overrated.

REX. The Klerat is a one-feed poison.

VIC. Nah – that's what it says on the box!

REX. It is – take it from me.

VIC. But I've got a tub-and-a-half of the Neo in the car.

REX. Well, use it up!

VIC. I'm trying, but there's a shortage of rats up my end.

REX. That's no excuse.

VIC. I'll give 'em a double-dose.

REX. No! – don't you waste it!

VIC. Trouble is, the more you give 'em, the less there are, the more you got, ad infinitem.

CHARMAINE. I really think a warm, milky drink'd be the best thing, Mr Weasel.

ROCK. Where's Mum?

REX. Where d'you think she is?

ROCK. I dunno.

REX. Where did we go for Christmas?

ROCK. Lanzarote.

REX. So – where's your mother?

ROCK. I dunno, do I? What're you doing here?

REX. I live here. What are you doing here? Ha, crafty bastard – caught yer! How d'you get in, eh? Who gave you the keys?

ROCK. Mum.

REX. Oh, did she? (*Pause.*) And don't you argue the toss with me, Maggott – you use the Klerat!

Exit ROCK.

REX. Where are you going? (*Follows him to the doorway.*) OI!!!!

The following whispered, quickly and inaudibly.

VIC. What're we goin' a do?

CHARMAINE. Well, I dunno – we can't leave that girl in there.

VIC. But it ain't got nothin' to do with us.

CHARMAINE. Vic, we can't – I'm not leavin' 'er – I'm not!

REX *is standing in the doorway, scrutinising them. They stop. Pause. Then –*

CHARMAINE (*aloud*). I 'ope she's going to be alright.

VIC. Yeah, 'course she is! She's full o' beans! (*Pause.*) Well, if everything's ginger-peachy with you, then, Boss, inasmuch you're clear about it, we'll be off . . .

CHARMAINE. Yeah . . .

VIC. 'Cos the truth is, it isn't what it ain't, 'cos it ain't what it isn't; inasmuch it ain't what it looks like, 'cos it ain't. 'Cos it is what it is, and it ain't what it ain't. Is it? Charmaine?

CHARMAINE. Yeah – no!

Pause. REX *continues his silent scrutiny.* VIC *makes several abortive attempts to start walking out of the room. These are vaguely echoed by* CHARMAINE. *Eventually . . .*

CHARMAINE. So, you just got back tonight, then, Mr Weasel. It's tiring, 'plane-travel, ain't it? I find it.

VIC. Yeah, I bet Rex wants to get to 'is bed – ain't that right, boss?

REX (*going to bed*). Yes, it is.

> *During the following,* REX *now puts down his airgun and his drink, and proceeds to prepare his bed by pounding and paddling the pillows. When this is finished, he sits on the bed, and takes off his shoes.*

VIC. I reckon you've got a touch of the old jet-lag syndrome, inasmuch as it catches up with you; specially on long-'ops, across the Equator to Australia and such: you can arrive before you've left.

> CHARMAINE *giggles.*

VIC. It disturbs your equilibrium. (*Pause.*) Alright, then, boss? If everything's hundred per cent with you, then, inasmuch tickety-boo, we'll be on our way!

CHARMAINE. Remember, that time we come back from Torremolinos, Vic? We was sleepin' nearly all the next day, wan' we?

VIC. Yeah, we was; but that was more to do with the grub and the grog, wan'it?

CHARMAINE. That's right! I was talking stupid then, as well, wan' I?

VIC. Yeah, we was, yeah!!

CHARMAINE (*laughs. Pause*). Are you going to bed, then, Mr Weasel?

REX (*aggressive*). Yes, I am going to bed. Any objections?

CHARMAINE (*good-humoured*). No! I wouldn't mind going to bed myself!

VIC. No need for that, Rex: she's only showin' a bit of concern.

CHARMAINE. It's alright, Vic.

VIC. What?

CHARMAINE. What's she doin'? (*She goes to the bathroom door, and taps on it.*) Listen, darlin': you can't stay in there all night. You've got to come out. What's the matter, eh? You can tell me. (*The rest of this speech from this point is delivered quietly, intimately, and almost inaudibly*). We're pals, ain't we? Mmm? Eh? Remember, we was 'avin' a laugh a few minutes ago – remember? Come on, darlin'. What you goin' a do in there

all night? You won't be able to eat nothin'. Ain't you 'ungry?
Eh? (*Pause*.) 'Ere – what about your Mum? Won't she be
worryin' about you? Eh? (*Pause*.) Listen, darlin' – I know you
think it's a mad'ouse out 'ere, don't yer? Mm? But . . . if you
come out, I'll protect you. I will. (*Pause*.) Honest. Eh? D'you
need anything? I've got some Nurofen in my bag – would
you like one? Please, darlin' – why don't you just come up to
the glass and talk to me? Eh? (*Pause*.) Listen, darlin' . . . it'll
really make my night if you come over 'ere. Come on, come
and talk to me – please. Just for me. Mm?

REX. Is she coming out?

*The following dialogue runs simultaneously with the preceding speech,
and starts when* CHARMAINE *begins to talk quietly.*

VIC. You got a callus there, Rex?

REX. No, Golfer's Foot.

VIC. Ooh, that sounds nasty. I 'ad a verruca once, when I was a
kid. My Mum made me burn my plimsolls.

REX. Did she? That must've stunk.

VIC. They did a bit; they was my big brother's. As a matter of
fact, they was 'is big brother's before that. (*Pause*.) Come to
think of it, I've got a vague recollection my sister wore 'em
one summer. (*Pause*.) I 'ope you didn't get the wrong end of
the stick there, Rex . . . inasmuch when the cat's away, the
mice do play, inasmuch ignorance is bliss, da!! (*Pause*.)
Course, they're a bad design, ain't they, feet? They weren't
built to take the weight of the body in a vertical position;
they was designed to be used in tandem, with the hands, like
a quadruped, scurrying and foraging in the bracken, in a
position, thus. But, what with the Ascent of Man, inasmuch
Evolution, 'e is now able to reach 'igh kitchen units, and
change electric light-bulbs, without the use of too 'igh a step-
ladder. Whereas once, we was as common as the Lowly
Iguana, crawlin', with a vegetarian bent.

REX. Is she coming out?

CHARMAINE. I'm sorry, I'm doin' my best.

REX. Well, get on with it!

CHARMAINE. Alright, Mr Weasel!

VIC. She's 'avin' a go, Rex!

Pause.

CHARMAINE (*normal audibility*). 'Ello, darlin'! Now . . . can you
'ear me? If you can 'ear me, tap your foot.

VIC. That's good. (*Pause.*) Anything?

CHARMAINE. I dunno . . .

REX. This is bloody stupid.

VIC. D'y'ave a nice 'oliday, Rex?

REX *glowers.*

VIC. Only, I've always thought it'd be good to go away for
Christmas. Save messin' up yer kitchen.

CHARMAINE (*laughing*). 'Ere – when was you ever in a kitchen,
Vic?

VIC. What about the giblets?

CHARMAINE. Well, you know me and giblets!

VIC. I know all about you and giblets!!

VIC *and* CHARMAINE *laugh uproariously.* REX *looks from one to
the other in total incomprehension.*

CHARMAINE. What was 'er name again?

VIC. I can't remember. Shall I ask your boy, boss?

REX. You can try.

VIC. Shall I?

REX. Go on.

VIC. I will.

Exit VIC. REX *yawns a big yawn, for a moment forgetting*
CHARMAINE.

VIC (*off, to* ROCK). Eh?

REX *remembers* CHARMAINE, *and throws her a suspicious glance.
She is still looking at* MELANIE-JANE. VIC *returns.*

VIC. Nothing.

REX. Typical. Now what?

CHARMAINE. Just a minute. (*Pause.*) What . . . Is . . . Your . . . Name? Mmm? (*Pause.*) I'll tell you what . . . I'll make a little deal with you: if I tell you my name, will you tell me yours? Mm?

VIC. The police do this.

CHARMAINE. My name's Charmaine. (*Sings.*) I wonder why you keep me waiting, (REX *grabs his gun, and jumps up, defensively.*) Charmaine cries, in vain.
I wonder when bluebirds are mating,
Will you come back again?

I wonder, if I keep on praying,
Will our dreams be the same?
I wonder if ever you think of me, too.
I'm waiting, my Charmaine, for you.

Pause.

VIC. That's nice, darlin'. Very soothing.

Long pause.

MELANIE-JANE (*off*). Melanie-Jane Beetles.

VIC. What's she say?

CHARMAINE. Melanie-Jane.

VIC. Yeah!

REX. Talk to 'er!

MELANIE-JANE (*off*). Beetles with two 'e's'. Like 'beetle'.

CHARMAINE. Oh, 'as it?

MELANIE-JANE (*off*). It hasn't got 'e.a.', like the Beatles. It's got two 'e's'. Everybody gets that wrong.

CHARMAINE. Do they?

MELANIE-JANE (*off*). They do. (*Pause.*) Where's Rocky?

CHARMAINE. What?

MELANIE-JANE (*off*). I want to know where Rocky is.

CHARMAINE. Oh, Rocky! 'E's in the sitting-room, I think.

VIC. No, 'e ain't.

CHARMAINE. In 'e?

VIC. Inasmuch 'e's in the scullery.

REX. Shut up, Maggott!!

MELANIE-JANE (*off*). That man's still there!

VIC. I'm goin' – tell 'er I'm goin'.

MELANIE-JANE (*off*). The man with the gun.

CHARMAINE. Oh, that's Mr Weasel. That's your boyfriend's Dad. He's a very nice man.

Pause.

MELANIE-JANE (*off*). I want to speak to Rocky, please.

CHARMAINE. I'll see what I can do, darlin' – don't you worry.

MELANIE-JANE (*off*). But I'm not coming out till that man's gone away. I'm not.

VIC. Medical shock can induce violence.

CHARMAINE. Are you getting the gist of this, Mr Weasel?

REX. Course I am. I'm not deaf. Right. Pay attention. This is the Battle Plan. One: I go in the lounge. Two: you tell her. Three: she comes out. Four: Rock comes in. Five: they talk. Understand?

CHARMAINE. Yes, Mr Weasel.

REX. Got that, Maggott?

VIC. Affirmative, boss.

REX (*momentarily suspicious*). Good. Tell her. (*Exit.*) Rock! Rock!

VIC *rushes over to* CHARMAINE. *The following speeches run simultaneously.*

REX (*off, loudly*). Go and talk to her. (*Pause.*) What're you waiting for? Get in there!

VIC (*inaudibly*). Charmaine; Charmaine! We've got to get out of 'ere. Charmaine, come on! It's nothing to do with us – it's 'is responsibility.

CHARMAINE (*inaudibly*). Listen, darlin', 'e's gone in the other room 'cos Rocky's in there – Vic, just a minute! Ssh! 'E's comin' to talk to you, darlin', so there's nothin' to worry about – Vic!

The following is heard by VIC *and* CHARMAINE, *who have stopped talking.*

REX (*off*). Right! You great lump! Pull yourself together, and bloody well get on with it!!!

REX thrusts ROCK into the room, and disappears off, mumbling. VIC and CHARMAINE rush over to ROCK.

CHARMAINE. You alright, darlin'?

VIC. Cor', 'e's a right old bastard, ain't 'e?

CHARMAINE. Don't let 'im walk all over you like that!

VIC. If my old man did that to me, I'd pull 'is eyes out with a corkscrew.

CHARMAINE. It's 'umiliatin'.

VIC. It ain't on.

CHARMAINE. She's very badly shaken up, your little girl.

VIC. Yeah – she's asked for you specifically.

CHARMAINE. You're needed, that's what you are!

VIC. She wants a bit of kindness –

CHARMAINE. That's right.

VIC. – Inasmuch warmth and affection.

CHARMAINE. Come on – use your instincts.

VIC. Yeah – go on.

CHARMAINE. But you've got to be quick about it!

VIC. You're 'er only link with reality.

CHARMAINE. That's right.

VIC. Inasmuch you're the light at the end of 'er tunnel. You're 'er only salvation. She's . . . she's like a lemming, teetering on the edge of the cliff; you've got to reach out your 'and, grab 'old of 'er tail, and drag 'er back!

CHARMAINE. Are you sure you're goin' a be alright?

VIC. Yeah – course 'e will . . . won't yer?

ROCK (*no response*).

VIC. There y'are! Look at 'im: fine, big, strappin' fella!

CHARMAINE. We'll be prayin' for you.

VIC. She will; I won't – I'm an agnostic.

> CHARMAINE *laughs uproariously*.

VIC. Anyway, God bless; Merry Christmas; nice to 'ave met you; good will to all men, inasmuch persons; and Auld Lang Syne.

CHARMAINE. And tell 'er Charmaine was askin' for 'er.

VIC. You've got a right little cracker there.

CHARMAINE. We'll be waiting for our invitations to the wedding, won't we, Vic?

VIC (*good-humoured*). Shut up, Charmaine!

> CHARMAINE *laughs*.

> *Enter* REX.

REX. What's going on?

VIC. We was just goin' 'ome, Rex.

CHARMAINE. Thank you very much, Mr Weasel.

VIC. If it's alright with you, we'll be making tracks.

CHARMAINE. Yeah.

REX. She's still in there!

CHARMAINE. Is she?

VIC. Oh, yeah!

> *Exit* VIC *and* CHARMAINE.

REX. Listen, fairy: get your playmate out of my bog!!!

> *Exit* REX.

> *During the following offstage dialogue,* ROCK *stands and looks at the bathroom door. Eventually,* MELANIE-JANE *opens it slightly, and gestures to* ROCK *through the gap. Then she opens it a little further, and hovers on the threshold. Thus they gaze at each other helplessly across the room.*

REX (*off*). Oi, you two! Sit down!

VIC (*off*). 'Ow d'you mean, Rex?

REX (*off*). Make yourselves at home!

CHARMAINE (*off*). It's alright – really, Mr Weasel.

REX (*off*). Right, Mrs Maggott, you'll have a sherry. What do you want, Vic?

VIC (*off*). No, it's alright, Rex.

REX (*off*). Scotch, Bourbon, Rye?

VIC (*off*). Got any whisky?

REX (*off*). Yes!

CHARMAINE (*off*). I thought we was goin' 'ome, Vic.

VIC (*off*). No, it's alright, Rex – really, yeah, three's a crowd, five's a rabble.

CHARMAINE (*off*). I have to be up early in the morning, Mr Weasel.

REX (*off*). One sherry, one Scotch.

CHARMAINE (*off*). No thankyou, Mr Weasel.

REX (*off*). Go on, you'll like it. Here you are, Vic.

VIC (*off*). Well, that's very civil of you, Rex, under the circumstances.

REX (*off*). Here's your sherry.

CHARMAINE (*off*). Are you having a drink, Vic?

VIC (*off*). We'll 'ave one for the road – eh?

CHARMAINE (*off*). Well, I'll have one if you're having one, but I shouldn't mix my drinks.

REX (*off*). Right: Merry Bloody Christmas!!

VIC (*off*). Chin-chin!

Pause.

CHARMAINE (*off*). I think boys get on better with their Mums, Mr Weasel, don't you? I mean, Vic, 'e gets on better with 'is Mum.

VIC (*off*). I do.

REX (*off*). Do you?

VIC (*off*). Yeah, I do.

CHARMAINE (*off*). I feel sorry for young people these days, though, Mr Weasel. There's not enough places for them to go. And I don't think we communicate enough with them, d'you know what I mean? I watch 'Top of the Pops' every Thursday night so's I've got something to say to my niece and nephew – it's like a labour of love with me, d'you know what I mean?

VIC (*off*). My wife is an acute observer of the Human Animal . . . inasmuch she is a student of the University of Life.

CHARMAINE (*off*). I'm not smart nor nothing, but I do know a thing or two about people.

VIC (*off*). Yeah, she's an instinctive, inasmuch a man-watcher.

CHARMAINE (*off: laughs.*)

VIC (*off*). No, I know, not, not, er –

CHARMAINE (*off*). No, I know, I –

VIC (*off*). I know I'm the only man you ever wanna watch.

CHARMAINE (*off*). Oh, that's what you think!

VIC (*off: laughs loudly and uproariously.*)

REX (*off*). Shut up, Maggot!!!! (*Pause.*) Go and see what's going on in there, will you?

MELANIE-JANE *hears this, and runs back into the bathroom, without closing the door.*

CHARMAINE (*off*). Are you talking to me, Mr Weasel?

REX (*off*). Yes. If you wouldn't mind.

CHARMAINE (*off*). I'll do that for you.

Enter CHARMAINE. *Only mouthing her words, she conducts a brief, friendly one-sided interview with* ROCK, *in which she ascertains his and* MELANIE-JANE's *condition, reassures him, and announces that she is going to close the door. She does this, giving him a conspiratorial wink on the way out.*

ROCK *stands motionless, looking at the bathroom. Pause.*
MELANIE-JANE *appears, and rushes across the room into his arms.*
She does this with such velocity that she almost knocks him over. Pause.
He turns round, and keeping his eye fixed on the door, he backs away
from it with MELANIE-JANE *still hugging him, like a koala-bear or*
a leech. Pause. MELANIE-JANE *now hugs him more passionately,*
and buries her head in his chest. She sinks to the floor, and hugs one of
his legs caressing it fervently for a while. Then she climbs up him
gradually, eventually (when she is standing) putting her arms round
him; he doesn't respond, so she puts his arms round her, one after the
other. Suddenly, they kiss, passionately, uninhibitedly, mutually; then,
just as suddenly, ROCK *pulls away.* MELANIE-JANE *rushes about*
the room like an uncoiled spring, whilst ROCK *watches the door.*
Then, again suddenly, they come back together embracing and kissing –
a long, passionate kiss. For a moment, they stop, and ROCK *picks up*
MELANIE-JANE, *sweeping her off the floor, and bears her to the*
bed, on to which they both sink, resuming their kiss. MELANIE-
JANE *stops kissing for a moment.*

MELANIE-JANE. Just a minute . . .

She takes off her glasses. They resume their kiss. Pause. Enter REX
. . .

The following dialogue runs simultaneously with the above action,
starting as CHARMAINE *rejoins* REX *and* VIC, *having closed the*
door.

REX *(off)*. What's going on?

CHARMAINE *(off)*. It's alright.

REX *(off)*. Has she come out?

CHARMAINE *(off)*. Yeah.

REX *(off)*. Is the door open?

CHARMAINE *(off)*. Yeah.

REX *(off)*. Right – we'll give 'em a couple o'minutes.

Pause.

CHARMAINE *(off)*. This is a nice sherry, Mr Weasel.

REX *(off)*. Yeah, yeah – it's a good one.

VIC *(off)*. Ditto the Scotch.

CHARMAINE (*off*). We nearly drunk all our Christmas drink, in't we, Vic?

VIC (*off*). Yeah, we 'ave – put a 'ole in it, 'aven't we?

CHARMAINE *laughs (off)*.

Pause.

VIC (*off*). I don't know why, but Christmas always makes me think of the War.

CHARMAINE (*off*). Why's that, Vic?

VIC (*off*). I dunno – I weren't in it or nothing; I ain't old enough.

CHARMAINE (*off*). Yeah . . . you seen it on telly, though.

VIC (*off*). I've seen it on telly. I've read a lot about it.

CHARMAINE (*off*). Yeah. Vic loves 'is books, Mr Weasel.

VIC (*off*). I do, yeah . . . yeah. (*Pause.*) No, it's all the old people down the market when I was a kid. They used to talk about it like it was still 'appening . . . they made me feel like I was in the Blitz.

CHARMAINE (*off*). I'm glad you wasn't, Vic.

VIC (*off*). Yeah, so'm I. (*Pause.*) Then, of course, there was old Lord Ha-Ha, wasn't there?

CHARMAINE (*off*). Oh, yeah . . .

VIC (*off*). Yeah. 'E was an Englishman, living in Germany, and working for the German BBC. Broadcasting propaganda to the Home Front . . . (*Imitating William Joyce, not very accurately.*) 'Germany calling! Germany calling! Mrs Smith! Do not send Johnny to the War! Keep him at home, tied to your apron strings . . .' That's 'ow 'e used to go on. 'Otherwise he will be crushed by the Might of the Reich!' Then, of course, a lot of young men went into the Black Market.

CHARMAINE (*off*). That's right.

VIC (*off*). Selling stockings; instead of fighting in the trenches.

CHARMAINE (*off*). Ow'd they know which Mrs Smith 'e was talkin' to?

VIC (*off*). Well, 'e wasn't talking to A Mrs Smith in particular, inasmuch as it's the way we would say, 'Mrs Schmidt.'

CHARMAINE (*off*). Oh, yeah.

> *Pause.*

VIC (*off*). Course, a lot o' people used to sleep in the tube-stations, didn't they?

CHARMAINE (*off*). That's right. Shelterin'.

VIC (*off*). Yeah.

CHARMAINE (*off*). Done a lot o' singing down there.

VIC (*off*). They did, yeah – 'eld 'em together. But it was very inconvenient for the traveller; gettin' out of the train, steppin' on their 'eads . . .

> *Pause.*

CHARMAINE (*off*). Yeah . . .

VIC (*singing, off*). Run, rabbit, run rabbit,
> Run, run, run . . .

CHARMAINE (*off*). That's right, Vic. They'll be alright, Mr Weasel.

> *Pause.*

VIC (*off*). Course, if there was a war now, it'd be different, wouldn't it? Be nucelar.

CHARMAINE (*off*). Yeah.

VIC (*off*). Be nothing left . . . unless o' course they dropped the neutron bomb.

CHARMAINE (*off*). Oh, I don't think Mr Weasel wants to hear about that, Vic!

VIC (*off*). That's the bomb that kills people but saves property . . . and clothing.

> REX, *who has not been listening to any of this, now enters the bedroom;* ROCK *and* MELANIE-JANE *are too involved to notice him. Short pause.*

REX. You cheeky buggers!!

> ROCK *leaps off the bed.* MELANIE-JANE *sits up.*

REX. Well, well, well!!! If it wasn't my bed you were on, I'd apologise. Are you going to introduce me? I'm Rocky's

Daddy! (*Pause.*) And this is my bedroom.

MELANIE-JANE (*getting up*). It's a very big bedroom, Mr Weasel.

REX. I'm glad you like it. (*He picks up her glasses.*) These yours?

MELANIE-JANE. Thank you very much. (*Pause.*) I'm very sorry . . .

REX. Well?

ROCK (*no response*).

REX. Does he talk to you? He never says a flaming word to me. He hasn't said a dicky-bird since the day he was born. Still . . .

> VIC *and* CHARMAINE *have appeared in the doorway.* VIC *knocks on the door, pom-diddly-om-pom; pom-pom.*

VIC. 'Scuse me, Rex; only me and Charmaine was thinkin' about wending our weary way. (*Pause.*) And by dint of farewell, I'd just like to say, 'Thankyou very much for all your 'ospitality.' Which, under the circumstances, was completely unwarranted, what with all the various disturbances. So, Thankyou Very Much. (*Pause.*) 'Appy Christmas. (Although it's almost over.) H'au revoir, inasmuch, Goodbye . . .

CHARMAINE. We don't want to outstay our welcome. 'Cos it is a family time, Christmas, init?

VIC. Yeah, it is, yeah. (*Pause.*) Er . . .

CHARMAINE. You're lookin' a lot better, ain't she, Vic?

VIC. Yeah, got a bit of colour back in your cheeks.

CHARMAINE. She's got a lovely smile!

VIC. She's a pretty girl, ain't she?

CHARMAINE. Yeah. (*To* ROCK.) You done a good job there.

VIC. Yeah, well done! 'Andsome young couple, ain't they?

CHARMAINE. Yeah.

> *Pause.*

VIC. Er . . . sh' we . . .?

CHARMAINE. ⎱ Yeah.
VIC. ⎰ Yeah.

CHARMAINE. Ba-bye.

VIC. Bye, then.

CHARMAINE. Ba-bye.

MELANIE-JANE. Bye-bye.

VIC. 'T's alright, we'll see ourselves out, Rex.

Exit VIC *and* CHARMAINE. *Pause. Then* REX *goes to the door.*

REX. Oi! Maggott!! Come back 'ere a minute!!

He stays at the door for a moment, then returns to where he was. Pause. VIC *appears.*

VIC. What's up, Rex? Found someone in the cupboard? (*Laughs.*)

REX. How long were you in prison, Vic?

Pause.

VIC. What're you talkin' about? That was 'undreds o' years ago.

REX. What did they get you for, G.B.H.?

VIC. Nah! Any'ow, it wasn't prison, inasmuch as it was Borstal.

REX. Oh, was it?

VIC. Yeah!

REX. Well, what were you doing, then, nicking motors?

VIC. Nah!

CHARMAINE. Vic was framed, Mr Weasel.

REX. I'm sure he was!

CHARMAINE. He was!

VIC. I bleedin' was! I fell in with a bad lot, inasmuch they took me for a mug; told me they was out for a laugh, ended up burnin' down a ware'ouse, inasmuch three hundred thousand poundsworth of fur coats.

CHARMAINE. Yeah – Vic was left alone to take the rap. And 'e didn't get no 'elp from 'is Dad, neether.

VIC. Dead right!

REX. Why don't I know about this?

VIC. With all due respects, boss, it ain't none of your bleedin' business!

CHARMAINE. I think that's Vic's own personal concern, Mr
  Weasel.

REX. Did they put you inside, as well?

CHARMAINE. I beg your pardon?

REX. You do have a criminal record?

CHARMAINE. I do not!

VIC. Now 'ang on a minute, Rex! You're takin' bleedin' liberties.
  You can 'ave a go at me, 'cos I work for yer, but you leave
  my missis out o' this!!

REX. Did you enjoy my chocolate, Mrs Maggott?

VIC. What?!

  Pause.

CHARMAINE. Now, look 'ere, Mr Weasel.

REX. Yes?

CHARMAINE. I've 'ad just about enough of this.

REX. Oh, have you?

CHARMAINE. I have, I'm not one to speak out of turn, but I
  'ave to say something. We've been made fools of, Vic an' me.
  We come 'ere tonight with the best of intentions. We live a
  quiet life. We work all the year round for not very much
  money; and, come Christmas, we like to enjoy ourselves, 'ave
  a few drinks and a laugh. We've been to one party . . . I
  know I was talkin' stupid, but we all do when we've 'ad a
  few.

VIC. Course we do.

CHARMAINE. But I do not see why we 'ave to be treated like
  little kids!

VIC. It's alright, darlin' – don't get yourself upset.

CHARMAINE. I'm alright, Vic. We've been led up the garden
  path like lambs to the slaughter, we 'ave. Let's go, Vic.

  CHARMAINE *starts to exit.*

REX. Alright I believe you – thousands wouldn't.

VIC. Good! 'Cos you should; 'cos it's the whole truth; the 'ole truth, and nothing but the truth! And that's 'ow it stands!

REX. Alright, don't you start sounding off, as well!

CHARMAINE. Leave it, Vic.

VIC. Eh?

REX (*to* ROCK). WHAT ARE YOU STARING AT??!!

VIC. Why don't you fuckin' leave 'im alone, you big bully?!

CHARMAINE. Vic!!

Pause.

REX (*quietly*). Watch your mouth, Vic. (*Pause.*) Now, I appreciate your coming round here this evening.

VIC. Oh, do yer?!

REX. Yes, I do. And you'll find a token of my appreciation in your pay packet at the end of the month.

VIC. What's that, me cards?

REX. No, a little extra.

VIC. Extra what?

REX. Extra money.

Pause.

VIC. Nah. No, that ain't necessary, Rex.

REX. I know it's not.

VIC. Nah. No, you're . . . you're well out of order, Rex.

REX. You scratch my back, I'll scratch yours.

CHARMAINE. Come on, Vic.

REX. When are you back at work, Vic?

VIC. Tuesday. Cockroaches in Colindale.

REX. Oh, yes. You can have a lie-in tomorrow.

VIC. Oh, thanks very much.

CHARMAINE. It's a Bank Holiday anyway, Vic.

VIC. Oh, yeah.

REX. Come on, I'll see you out.

CHARMAINE (*to the others*). Take care.

VIC. 'Bye.

MELANIE-JANE. Bye-bye.

> *Exit* REX, VIC *and* CHARMAINE. *During the following dialogue,* MELANIE-JANE *tries unsuccessfully to communicate with* ROCK.

VIC (*off*). Oh – yer keys.

REX (*off*). No, I don't want 'em – give 'em to Roy.

VIC (*off*). Fair enough.

REX (*off*). Mind how you drive.

VIC (*off*). No problem.

REX (*off*). The police are out.

VIC (*off*). I'm as sober as a judge.

REX (*off*). It's that time of year.

CHARMAINE (*off*). Gone nippy, init?

VIC (*off: opening front door*). 'Ere y'are, darlin'.

CHARMAINE (*off*). Goodnight, Mr Weasel.

REX (*off*). Goodnight, Mrs Maggott.

VIC (*off*). Goodnight, Rex.

REX (*off*). Goodnight, Vic.

VIC (*off*). 'Appy New Year!

> *The front door closes. Enter* REX. *He is still holding the airgun. Pause.*

REX. Any questions?

ROCK (*no response*).

REX. Eh?

> *Long pause.* REX *looks round the room, his attention eventually focusing on the soft animals on the floor. He stares at these violently for a long time. Then he stares at* ROCK. ROCK *stares back. Then –*

ROCK. WHAT?!!

Pause. Then REX *moves quickly towards the bathroom;* MELANIE-JANE *jumps out of his way.*

MELANIE-JANE. Don't – !!!

REX *goes into the bathroom, and reappears with his dressing-gown and his toilet-bag. He puts them on the bed. He puts the gun on the bed. He goes to the chest of drawers, and takes out a pair of pyjamas which he puts on the bed. He goes out, and returns with a full bottle of Scotch whisky . He sits on the bed, and puts on his shoes. During this –*

MELANIE-JANE. It makes you burp . . . whisky. (*Pause.*) It's a shame you can't walk home anymore. It's not safe. But then it might not really be safe getting a taxi, either. You could get raped . . .

REX *has put on his shoes, and now goes to one of the wardrobes, and takes out a leather overnight bag – not part of the luggage he arrived with. He takes this to the bed, and proceeds to pack.*

MELANIE-JANE. Are you going back to Lanzarote, Mr Weasel?

REX *finishes the packing, and zips up the bag. Then he goes to 'his' wardrobe, takes out the raincoat he arrived in, and proceeds to put it on.*

MELANIE-JANE. That's a nice raincoat, Mr Weasel. Hasn't your Daddy got a nice raincoat, Rocky?

ROCK (*no response*).

MELANIE-JANE. Sensible coat.

REX *takes a huge wad of paper money out of his back pocket. He flicks through it.*

REX. D'you need any money?

ROCK (*no response*).

Pause. REX *glances at* MELANIE-JANE, *incidentally.*

MELANIE-JANE. No, thankyou.

REX *ignores this. He counts out some money, and puts it on the bed, under the airgun.*

REX. A hundred quid. (*He goes to the door.*) Have fun.

Exit REX, *closing the door. The front door slams.* MELANIE-JANE *runs to* ROCK, *and stands beside him. Pause.*

MELANIE-JANE. Was that the front door? (*Pause.*) Was it? (*Pause.*)
He's hiding – he hasn't gone anywhere. (*Pause. She goes to the
door and listens.*) Can't hear anything. (*She opens the door, and
creeps into the hall; after a moment, she returns.*) There's nobody
here at all. (*Pause, she sits on the bed.*) I thought he was really
going to kill us. He left you all that money. (*Pause.*) It's gone
all quiet.

> ROCK *crosses the room. He stands for a short while, and then crosses
> back.* MELANIE-JANE *goes out of the room, and returns with her
> coat and her handbag, which she puts on the bed. She proceeds to put
> on her coat.*

MELANIE-JANE. My Daddy will murder me. (*Pause.*) What are
you going to spend your hundred pounds on? Where is she,
your Mummy? What's the matter?

> ROCK *moves to the dressing-table, and stares at it.*

MELANIE-JANE. You'd better put it somewhere safe. (*Pause.*) Do
you like me? (*Pause.*) Are you going to stay here tonight? I
bet my Daddy will be in bed by now. No-one will know what
time I get in. (*Pause.*) It's a good thing we haven't got a dog.
(*Pause.*) Rocky . . .

> ROCK *puts on his coat, takes his cassette out of the radio/cassette
> player and puts it back in his Walkman.*

MELANIE-JANE. Rocky – what are you doing?

> *Exit* ROCK, *quickly. He leaves the flat.*

MELANIE-JANE. Where are you going? (*She follows him to the door.*)
What's wrong? (*She rushes back to get her bag, and rushes out.*)
Don't go! What about your money? – Rocky: WAIT! (*Off.*)
You've left the lights on! (*The front door slams. We hear her beyond
it.*) Wait for me! Please . . .!

> *Long pause. Slow fade to blackout.*

The End

ECSTASY

Characters

JEAN
ROY
DAWN
VAL
LEN
MICK

Jean and Dawn are natives of Birmingham. Mick is from County Cork, Len is from rural Lincolnshire and Roy and Val are from inner North London, where the play is set. The dialogue, language and usage in *Ecstasy* are extremely precise, and in the author's view the play should only be performed in the correct accents.

Time: 1979

Ecstasy was first performed at the Hampstead Theatre, London, on 19 September 1979 with the following cast:

JEAN   Sheila Kelley
ROY   Ron Cook
DAWN   Julie Walters
VAL   Rachel Davies
LEN   Jim Broadbent
MICK   Stephen Rea

Directed by Mike Leigh
Designed by Alison Chitty
Costumes by Lindy Hemming
Lighting by Alan O'Toole

ACT ONE

Scene One

JEAN's *bedsitting room in Kilburn. Bleak. Cramped. Kitchen within the room, concealed behind crude wall-partition, in doorway of which is old, disused 'Marley' folding door. Main room entered through kitchen. Furniture all drab, second-hand. Single bed, wardrobe (kept closed), small armchair, table (more cluttered than used), two chairs (one by the table, one serving as a bed-side table), bed-side lamp, alarm-clock, one-bar electric fire, mirror, old television set (in little-used position), old record-player, old transistor radio, paperback books, newspapers, box of chocolates, empty bottles, candle in wine bottle, cigarette packets, matches, some dead flowers in a jug, odds and ends. In the kitchen, an old 'Baby Belling' electric cooker, small sink, 'Sadia' (or similar) electric water heater, electricity meter, electric kettle, pans, shelves, garbage-bin, tins of food, culinary odds and ends.*

Night, winter.

Lights up.

JEAN *and* ROY, *stark naked on the bed.* JEAN *is lying on her back.* ROY *is sitting sideways on the bed, with his back to her. Neither moves.*

Pause.

ROY *picks up a packet of cigarettes, and takes one out.*

ROY. Wanna fag?

JEAN. Yeah.

 ROY *gives her a cigarette, then lights the cigarettes, his own first.*

ROY. Good that, wannit?

JEAN. Yeah.

 ROY *gets up, goes to the table, picks up an opened can of beer, and finishes it off in one. Then he puts on his underpants, takes a fresh can of beer out of a carrier-bag, and opens it.*

ROY. You want one of these?

JEAN. No.

JEAN gets dressed. ROY drinks.

ROY belches.

JEAN makes the bed. Then she picks up an almost-empty Martini bottle from the floor near the bed, pours the last drop into an empty glass, and puts the bottle back on the floor.

ROY gets dressed.

JEAN sits in the armchair.

JEAN. I 'ate the winter.

ROY. Still cold, are you?

JEAN. Yeah – ain't you?

ROY. Me? No.

JEAN puts on a cardigan.

ROY is finishing tying his shoelaces. He glances at his watch.

JEAN. What's the time?

ROY. Ten past nine.

JEAN gets up and goes into the kitchen.

JEAN. I'll put the kettle on.

She does so.

Do you want a cup o' tea?

ROY finishes the can of beer.

Eh?

ROY adjusts his crutch.

D'you want a cup?

Pause.

You going?

ROY. Yeah, I got to shoot off.

JEAN. Why?

ROY. 'Cos I 'ave.

JEAN. Oh, sorry.

Pause.

ROY. 'Ere, you can 'ave them.

JEAN. What?

ROY. Some beers left.

JEAN. Thanks.

ROY. Tara. 'Ere – 's a good job your friend didn't turn up, eh?

JEAN. Well, it's still early yet, 'er still might come.

ROY. Yeah, well. See you.

> ROY *leaves.*

> JEAN *takes an unopened can of beer out of the carrier-bag, and puts several empty cans and the Martini bottle into the carrier-bag, which she puts by the garbage can in the kitchen. She unplugs the kettle. Then she goes to the wardrobe, opens it, gets out a new bottle of Martini, and puts that on the table. Then she closes the wardrobe, and tops up her drink from the new bottle, which she puts on the floor where the old one was. She sits on the bed, and puts her glass on the chair by the bed. She gets the can of beer from the table, and puts that on the chair by the bed. She puts her feet up on the bed, and has a swig of Martini.*

Pause.

Blackout.

End of Scene One

Scene Two

Early evening, winter.

Lights up – dim: the room unlit.

JEAN *heard opening the front door. Children's voices heard in the street.*

DAWN (*off*). Tracy! Mind that bleedin' lamp-post, will ya? And keep away from that kerb! Told ya.

JEAN (*entering the room*). Init dark?

> JEAN *turns on the light.*

DAWN (*entering*). Listen to a word you bleedin' say they don't, Jean. Jean –

JEAN. Mm?

DAWN. Can I leave this door open a bit?

JEAN. Yeah, alright.

DAWN. Bleedin' cloth ears, them two, talk yourself stupid, you would.

JEAN. Been waitin' out there long, 'ave yer?

DAWN. No, no. I've 'ad 'em up to 'ere today, Jean, up to 'ere.

JEAN. 'Ave yer?

DAWN. I 'ave. Drove me mad. Blimey, it's parky, init?

JEAN. I'm just plugging the fire in.

DAWN. Been up Oxford Street today.

JEAN. 'Ave yer?

DAWN. Yeah. They'm buggers, y'see, Jean. Buggers! Murder comin' up the Kilburn 'Igh Road with them!

JEAN is offering DAWN a cigarette.

No, come on, 'ave one o'mine.

JEAN. 'Ere no, 'ave one o' these.

DAWN. Don't be so daft – come on.

JEAN. Go on. I've got them out now.

DAWN. Oh, go on, then. Jesus, 'er's got a mouth on 'er, Tracy. No discipline you see, Jean. What it is, no bleedin' discipline. 'E ain't no 'elp, neither – all on my back, you know.

JEAN is putting on the kettle in the kitchen.

JEAN. Mm.

DAWN. Jean . . .

JEAN. Aye?

DAWN. Fancy goin' out tomorrow night?

Pause.

JEAN. Yeah.

DAWN. Do ya?

JEAN. Yeah.

DAWN. Go for a drink, eh? Me and you?

JEAN. Yeah.

DAWN. Yeah. Thought we'd go to the 'Bell'.

JEAN. Mm.

DAWN. Yeah. 'E'll be there, mind.

JEAN. Will 'e?

DAWN. Oh, don't matter, though, Jean, don't 'ave to drink with 'im.

JEAN laughs.

Children's voices in street.

DAWN. 'Er upstairs'll baby-sit.

JEAN. Will 'er?

DAWN. Oh, ah. Better go an' check 'em, Jean, see if they'm alright – I couldn't mek it last night, you know.

DAWN is on the way out.

JEAN. No.

DAWN. No – wouldn't stop in, would 'e?

JEAN laughs.

Pause.

DAWN returns.

DAWN. 'Er's soaked, Michelle, y'know, needs changing. Ooh, Jean, I've 'ad a week of it with them two and that push-chair.

JEAN. 'Ave yer?

DAWN. They both want to push the babby now – both on 'em, Simone an' all – fighting, they've bin, told 'er, 'Tracy pushes the push-chair, not Simone. Tracy knows.' Don't like it, though, y'know, Simone – don't like bein' told. 'E bought 'er a little doll's pram, see, for 'er birthday, that's what started it, Jean.

JEAN. Oh, ah.

DAWN. Told 'er, 'Michelle ain't no doll. Proper babby. No doll.'

JEAN. Got a present for 'er 'ere.

    JEAN *gets out a paper bag.*

DAWN. Don't deserve no present, 'er, Jean.

JEAN. 'Ere y' are.

DAWN. You bought 'er?

JEAN. Paintin' book and some paints.

DAWN. 'Er ain't gettin' that tonight – you know what 'er's been doin', Jean?

JEAN. No.

DAWN. 'Er's only been goin' round at school tellin' everybody 'er Daddy's died. Daddy's died, Jean! Says, 'I'll give you died, Simone, give you died! – See if 'e's died when 'e comes in tonight!'

JEAN. 'E wouldn't like that, will 'e?

DAWN. 'E wouldn't like it, Jean! Thinks the sun shines out of 'er, 'e does. Favouritises 'er, see, t'ain't right. No, 'er was waitin' for me tonight, teacher at the school gates, when I went to pick 'em up – oh, ah: Miss Beaumont-Lewis. Said 'er was worried about Simone. I said, 'Oh, you're worried, am ya, worried?' I says, 'you wanna 'ave the three on 'em, then you'd be worried!' Said 'er was subvertive.

JEAN. Eh?

DAWN. Said Simone was subvertive.

JEAN. Perhaps somebody in the class, their Dad's died, 'er's just copying them.

DAWN. Must 'ave, Jean.

JEAN. Yeah, that'd be it.

DAWN. Must 'ave – they do that, see? 'M buggers. 'Ey – got yer a present.

JEAN. 'Ave yer?

DAWN. Yeah: top.

    DAWN *produces a brightly coloured 'top' – i.e. blouse etc.*

JEAN. Ooh.

DAWN. Lovely, init?

JEAN. Yes, 't's nice.

DAWN. Thought of you when I seen that, Jean. Got me one, an'
all.

JEAN. 'Ave yer?

DAWN (*producing an identical 'top'*). See?

JEAN. Oh, ah.

DAWN. Lovely, in't they?

JEAN. Yeah, nice colours, in't they?

DAWN. Eh? Ooh, ah! Seen this, Jean, I said, 'It's goin' on my
back, that is.'

JEAN. Did you buy 'em?

DAWN. 'Course I did – did I fuck! Did I buy 'em? Yer'm jokin',
in't ya?

JEAN. Yeah.

DAWN. Did I buy 'em! Got 'em up C & A. Don't buy nothin' in
C & A, you go in, 'elp yourself. See, got me a skirt, an' all.

JEAN. Oh, ah.

DAWN. Lovely, enit?

JEAN. Yeah, it's nice.

DAWN. See – it's got a pleat.

JEAN. Oh, ah.

DAWN. See what I mean, you can wear 'em together.

JEAN. Yeah. Yeah, it'll suit you, that.

DAWN. Ooh, ah. I 'ope they'll fit me, though, Jean. Ent tried 'em
on, you know. Tell ya – if these don't fit me, I'm takin' them
back.

JEAN. Ooh, blimey.

Pause.

DAWN. Been to work, 'ave ya?

JEAN. Yeah.

Pause.

DAWN. Busy, was ya?

JEAN. Yeah.

    Pause.

DAWN. Been doin' wi' yourself?

JEAN. Just goin' to work, and coming home, yer know . . .

DAWN. Ent yer been out nowhere?

JEAN. No.

DAWN. Ooh, Jean, that ent no good for ya.

JEAN. Oh well, suits me, that.

DAWN. You still ent got a bloke?

JEAN. No.

    JEAN *goes into the kitchen to make the tea.*

DAWN. Oh, Jean, you wanna get yourself a nice bloke, you do, get yourself took out.

JEAN. 'T's easier said than done, init?

DAWN. Oh, ar, I know. Never mind, Jean, go out tomorrow night, get yourself pissed.

    JEAN *laughs.*

    Did I tell yer Tracy got thrown out of Irish Dancing Class?

JEAN. No.

DAWN. Did, you know; last Sat'day.

JEAN. What for?

DAWN. Tell you what for, Jean – I'll tell you what 'er told me. 'Er was doin' the dancing, right?

JEAN. Mm.

DAWN. An' there was this little kid dancin' be'ind 'er, Mickey Lynch. Trod on 'er shoe, see? So, 'er come out o' the shoe, an' 'er couldn't do the dancin' proper, the teacher was goin' on at 'er. Jean: 'er only turned round an' punched 'im in the throat; called 'im an Irish cunt.

JEAN. Ooh dear.

DAWN. No, it's that Miss Beaumont-Lewis I can't stick, though, Jean. Can't stick 'er, I can't. Looks down on me – know what I mean?

JEAN. Yeah.

DAWN. Can tell. Thinks I don't know. Snob, 'er is. Wooden bleedin' earrings, Jean.

JEAN *gives* DAWN *a cup of tea.*

Ooh, lovely. Lovely, Jean. Ent you been out with nobody?

JEAN *is smuggling* ROY's *can of beer into the kitchen.*

JEAN. No, no. Old is 'er, that teacher?

DAWN. Eh? Oh, I don't know – 'er's older 'n' us. Int married, though, int got no babbies. Think they'm it, teachers.

JEAN *sits at the table with her tea.*

JEAN. Ooh, ah, they're all the same, int they?

DAWN. Ooh, ah.

JEAN. D'you remember Sister Boniface?

DAWN. Ooh, blimey, I do. I 'ated 'er, I did!

JEAN. And Mrs Malvern.

DAWN. Ooh, ar, 'er 'ated me.

JEAN. 'Er weren't too fond of me, either.

DAWN. 'Er worn't, was 'er? 'T's lovely, that top, though, init, Jean?

JEAN. Oh, yeah.

DAWN. You wanna wear that tomorrow night, you do.

JEAN. Yes.

DAWN. Do yourself up a bit.

JEAN. Oh, well, I'm alright, you know . . .

DAWN. No, you wanna enjoy yourself, you do, Jean.

JEAN. Yeah. Wanna fag?

DAWN. No, come on – 'ave one o' mine, 'ad one o' yourn.

JEAN. Is Mick workin'?

DAWN. Eh? Ooh, ah, 'e's workin' today, in 'e? Wunt workin' last Friday, though. Celebrating Simone's birthday, see, Thursday night.

JEAN. Ooh, ah.

DAWN. Gave 'er a bit of a party, I did. Got 'er a little cake, few candles for the top. Little Eamonn come down, from upstairs – Theresa bought 'er a bunny rabbit, Jean – bunny rabbit, an' 'er's six. Stupid – any road, Michelle went and dropped it down the toilet, 'ad to throw it out. Bumped 'er 'ead on that basin an' all again you know, Jean.

JEAN. Mm?

DAWN. 'S got bumps on 'er 'ead the size of eggs. You know that cupboard in our kitchen that don't shut?

JEAN. Yeah.

DAWN. Always goin' into it.

JEAN. Comes sharp that, an' all, dunnit?

DAWN. Ooh ah. Any road, as I say, 'e comes in, Jean, gives 'er 'er doll's pram, 'e goes out. Don't see 'im till three o'clock Friday morning. Wouldn't go to work then, see? Sat'day, twelve o'clock, Jimmy the Gimp comes round, they go out, don't see 'im till all hours Sunday morning; throwin' up everywhere 'e was, an' all. Said it was the curry! Y'know what I mean?

JEAN. Oh ah.

DAWN. Yeah – made me laugh, though, Jean. Couldn't get up the pub all day Sunday. Too poorly, see? Din't go in Monday, neither.

JEAN. Did yer get me card?

DAWN. Ooh ah. Got yer card, ah! 'Er were dead chuffed wi' that, Simone. Card? Auntie Jean? Ooh, ah. Should've come round over the weekend, Jean.

JEAN. Yeah. Yeah, well – I 'ad a lot to do, you know.

DAWN. Did yer? What was yer doin'?

JEAN. Well, I 'ad to clean the place up a bit. Give the 'all a bit of a scrub – Sunday's the only day you've got to do it, init?

DAWN. Ooh ah, I know, don't tell me. You doin' tonight?

JEAN. Well, probably watch the telly, 'ave a bath, give me 'air a bit of a wash, you know . . .

DAWN. Yeah. There's a funny smell in 'ere, you know, Jean.

JEAN. Of what?

DAWN. Dunno – 's a funny smell, though.

JEAN. It's probably the cigarettes.

DAWN. No – don't smell like cigarettes to me.

JEAN. Well, I can't smell anything.

DAWN. No, you live 'ere, don't ya?

JEAN. 'T's right.

DAWN. No – can't smell your own place, see? Should've got me some tights, an' all. 'T's alright that skirt, though, init, Jean?

JEAN. Yeah, 't's nice.

DAWN. They've got some gorgeous stuff in C & A, though.

JEAN. Yeah, good shop, C & A.

DAWN. Ooh, ah. Get you a skirt if you want, Jean.

JEAN. Well, I don't really need any skirts.

DAWN. Don't ya? Int yer been nowhere, Jean?

JEAN. No, no. Well, you can't go out on yer own, can yer?

DAWN. No, you can't, no. Think you'm on the make, don't they? Know what men'm like, Jean. Only after one bleedin' thing. Eh?

JEAN. Mm.

DAWN. Better be goin', any road.

JEAN. Yeah, got to get their teas.

DAWN. Yeah, beefburgers I've got 'em – Jesus, 'er's got an appetite on 'er, Tracy – 'er eats more'n 'e does, 'er does, Jean – size on 'er, an' all.

JEAN. 'Er's only thin, in' er?

DAWN. 'Er is. Worries me, you know, that does. Think 'er's got a worm, I do. I mean, look at Simone: 'er's well-rounded, Simone, 'er don't eat 'alf as much as Tracy – 'alf a pound of bleedin' sugar 'er put on 'er Sugar Puffs this morning, Jean, three spoons o' sugar in 'er tea, I say to 'er, 'You'll be gettin' sugar diabetes next, you.' No, I'll get 'em to bed, though, Jean, tomorra. Mind you, 'er's a bugger, Tracy, you know, she still ain't sleepin' proper.

JEAN. Per'aps 'er just don't need a lot o' sleep.

DAWN. No, 'er ain't like you. Think it's nerves, I do. Little bags under 'er eyes, 'n' all, y'know, I says, 'You'll be moaning about them when you'm eighteen – come to me wi' bags under your eyes an' no teeth!' Not 'avin' that tomorrow night, though, Jean: get 'em to bed. Mind you, they'll go to bed, you know what I mean, they'll go. They'm'll say their prayers every night, you know, Tracy and Simone, ooh ah, kneel down, 'God Bless Mummy, God Bless Daddy, God Bless Tracy, God Bless Simone, God Bless Michelle, God Bless Mickey Mouse, God Bless Auntie Jean,' you'm 'alf-way out o' the bleedin' door, Jean, and they'm up. Cunts. You fancy a night out, though, do ya?

JEAN. Oh, yeah. Yeah.

DAWN. You ain't been out wi' nobody?

JEAN. No. No – I ain't met anybody I've liked.

DAWN. Oh; ain't there no blokes down that garage, Jean?

JEAN. Well, only them I work with.

DAWN. Oh ah, they'm Pakis, ent they?

JEAN. Yeah.

DAWN. You don't want to be goin' out wi' them, Jean.

JEAN. Don't I?

DAWN (going out). You wanna get this door shut, Jean, get the flat warmed up a bit.

JEAN. Ar, I will.

JEAN sees DAWN to the hall

DAWN (*off*). Yeah. Pick you up tomorrow, Jean, eight-thirty: alright?

JEAN (*off*). Alright.

DAWN (*off*). Yeah. See where buggers've got to now.

JEAN (*off*). Tara a bit.

JEAN *comes back into the room.*

DAWN (*off*). Tara, Jean. Tracy! Come on, we'm going! Simone.

Children's voices. DAWN *closes the front door.*

JEAN *takes the evening newspaper and a fresh packet of cigarettes out of her shopping-bag, and puts the bag in the kitchen. Then she goes to the wardrobe, gets out a bottle of gin, and puts it on the table. She hangs the new 'top' on a clothes-hanger in the wardrobe. She closes the wardrobe. She puts the dirty tea-cups in the kitchen sink, out of which she takes a dirty glass. She washes this, comes back into the room, sits at the table, and pours herself a gin.*

She doesn't drink it. She doesn't do anything.

Pause.

Blackout.

End of Scene Two

Scene Three

Evening.

Lights up.

JEAN *is sitting on the bed, reading a newspaper. The bed-side lamp is on. She is wearing a different-coloured cardigan. Her feet are on the floor.*

She puts down the newspaper, and sits back on the bed, with her feet up. She picks up the clock, looks at it, and puts it back. (It's well after 9 o'clock.)

She gets up, goes into the kitchen, takes a dirty glass from the sink, washes and dries it, comes back into the room, gets a bottle of tonic water from the wardrobe, and pours herself a gin-and-tonic.

She stands sipping her drink. Then she lights the candle. Then she gets out a cigarette, and lights it from the candle.

Pause: she stands, looking at the candle.

Then she puts the cigarettes, the matches, and an ashtray by the armchair, gets her drink, sits down, and starts reading a paperback book. Then she kicks off her shoes.

The door-bell rings.

Pause.

JEAN *gets up and goes to the front door.*

ROY (*off*). Hullo, Jean. Thought I'd come round and see 'ow you was, you know?

JEAN (*off*). Yeah.

> *They come into the room.*

> Come in.

ROY. 'Ow are you, are you alright?

JEAN. Yeah, yeah, I'm alright, are you?

ROY. Want a fag?

JEAN. No, I've got one on, ta.

ROY. What's that you're drinking?

JEAN. Gin-and-tonic: d'you want one?

ROY. No thanks. Ain't there none of my beer left?

JEAN. Yeah.

> JEAN *gets* ROY's *can of beer from the kitchen.*

ROY. Ta.

> ROY *opens the beer.*

> 'Ow are you, are you alright?

> JEAN *is back in the kitchen, cleaning another glass.*

JEAN. Yeah, yeah. Glass 'ere.

ROY. Bit of a change, init, gin-and-tonic?

JEAN. Yeah – yeah, well, I like a change, sometimes.

> JEAN *sits back in the armchair.* ROY *sits on the bed.*
> *Pause.*

ROY. 'Ow yer been, alright?

JEAN. Yeah. You been up the pub?

ROY. Yeah, popped in for a couple, you know . . .

> *Pause.*

> You go out last night?

JEAN. No.

ROY. Oh, I should've come round. What you been doin', then?

JEAN. Just workin'. You still doin' that Indian Restaurant?

ROY. No, got shot of that.

JEAN. What you doin' now, then?

ROY. 'Ouse.

JEAN. Where?

ROY. Up in 'Ampstead. Big fuckin' palace of a place.

JEAN. Bet that's cold, init?

ROY. What?

JEAN. Paintin'.

ROY. No, we're doin' the insides. Do exteriors when they get back.

JEAN. Where they gone?

ROY. South Africa.

JEAN. Well, they must trust you, then, if they've left you there on your own.

ROY. Do they fuck. They'll 'ave someone round to keep an eye on us, relation or something.

> *Pause.*

> Wondered if you'd be in. You know . . .

JEAN. Yeah. Yeah – well I am.

ROY. Warm enough over there for you?

JEAN. Yeah. Yeah.

ROY. Still got the old candle on, then?

JEAN. Yeah. Saves the matches.

ROY. Burn the fuckin' place down, you will.

> *Pause. Then* ROY *gets up, and takes a swig of beer.*

ROY. Thought I'd come round 'n' see 'ow you was, you know.

JEAN. Yeah – well, I'm alright.

> ROY *picks up a book.*

ROY. Still readin' then?

JEAN. Yeah.

ROY. Fuckin' waste of time.

> *He throws the books on the bed. Then he sits on the corner of the bed, nearer to* JEAN.
>
> *Pause.*

JEAN *(getting up)*. I think I'll get a top-up.

ROY. You seen your friend?

JEAN. Yeah.

ROY. What, she turn up?

JEAN. No, 'er come yesterday. Why?

ROY. Oh, I wondered why she didn't come.

JEAN. Couldn't.

ROY. Why's that?

JEAN. Couldn't get a babysitter.

ROY. Oh, yeah: fuckin' kids.

JEAN *(sitting in the armchair)*. Don't seem to keep you in.

ROY. Eh? 'T's not my problem, is it?

JEAN. They're your kids.

ROY. I didn't fuckin' ask for them. What're them, then?

JEAN. Pistachio nuts – d'you want one?

ROY. No, thanks.

JEAN. Don't you like 'em?

ROY. No. What, are they sweet, are they?

JEAN. They're lovely – 'ave one.

ROY. No, they don't taste of nothing.

JEAN. 'Course they do.

ROY. Where d'you get 'em, then?

JEAN. Shop.

ROY (*rubbing* JEAN'*s leg*). Alright, are you?

JEAN. Yeah.

ROY. Get your legs burnt off, sittin' there.

JEAN. Oh, I don't care.

ROY. Goin' out the weekend?

JEAN. No. Are you?

ROY. Dunno yet. Might go up the Dogs. (*He takes the bag of pistachio nuts from* JEAN'*s lap.*) 'Ow much you pay for these, then?

JEAN. 75 pence.

ROY. Oh. Yeah. That's a lot, init, for peanuts?

JEAN. Well, they are expensive.

ROY (*tossing them back into her lap*). You've been done.

    Pause.

    You alright over there?

JEAN. Yeah – don't I look alright?

ROY. Come and sit over 'ere.

JEAN. No, I'm alright 'ere, I like it 'ere.

    Pause. Then ROY *gets up, goes over to the empty bottles, and checks through them.*

ROY. Got any more beer left?

JEAN. No.

ROY. What, no Guinness?

JEAN. No.

He picks up the new Martini bottle.

ROY. Is this the same bottle?

JEAN. Yeah.

ROY. Cor, I 'ate gin. (*Pouring himself a gin.*) Want another one?

JEAN. No. I've just 'ad one. But you 'ave one.

ROY. Ta. Cheers.

ROY *lights a cigarette. He swigs his gin. He sits on the bed.*

ROY. 'Ere y'are, come on.

JEAN. No, I'm alright 'ere.

ROY *clears a newspaper off the bed.*

ROY. Still cold, are yer?

JEAN. Well, 't ain't warm, is it?

ROY *clears the book off the bed.*

ROY. 'Ere y'are: come and sit over 'ere.

JEAN. No.

ROY *gets up. He moves over to* JEAN, *and leans over her.*

ROY. Alright, are you?

JEAN. Yeah. Yeah.

ROY. You sure?

JEAN. Yeah. Mm.

ROY. 'Ere y'are, come and sit over 'ere.

He moves her across to the bed. They sit on the bed, side by side.

ROY. That's better, init?

JEAN. Yeah.

He kisses her, briefly. Then he caresses her hair, slightly brutally. She takes a sip of her drink. He takes her glass from her, and puts it on the table.

He rubs her back.

ROY. Alright, are you?

JEAN. Yeah.

He kisses her again, and they lie down together, whilst continuing to kiss. Then JEAN *sits up abruptly.*

JEAN. Look, um, I don't really feel like it.

ROY. What's the matter?

JEAN. Well, I just don't feel like it.

ROY. Why?

JEAN. 'Cos I don't.

ROY. 'Course you do.

He forces her down again. He kisses her. He fondles her breasts. She turns her head away from him.

JEAN. No!!

ROY (*persisting*). What's the matter with you?

He sits up.

Bit of a change of tune, init?

Pause.

'S alright the other nights, wonnit? Eh?

JEAN. Yeah. Yeah.

Pause.

ROY. You wanna drink?

JEAN. Yeah.

He goes to the table, and pours some drinks. She sits up. He gives her a drink.

JEAN. Ta.

ROY. I was goin' to bring some beers.

Long pause.

'Ere y'are, come on: get it down yer. (*He tries to take her glass from her, but she holds on to it.*)

JEAN. 'Aven't finished it yet.

ROY *lights a cigarette.*

JEAN *gets up suddenly, puts down her drink, and quickly takes off her cardigan.*

JEAN. Come on, then.

> JEAN *lies on the bed on her back.* ROY *takes off his shirt, puts out his cigarette, and sits on the bed.*

JEAN *(as he sits).* Let's get it over with.

ROY. What's your fuckin' game, eh?

JEAN. Gerroff me!

ROY. Eh? What're you playin' at?

JEAN. Gerroff.

> *They struggle for some time, with increasing violence.*
>
> *Eventually* ROY *jumps up.*

ROY. What the fuck's the matter with you?

> *Pause.*
>
> ROY *sits in the armchair.*

ROY. Fuckin' bitches, you're all the bleedin' same. You wannit, then you don't wannit.

> *He lights a fresh cigarette.*

Wanna fag?

> *Pause.*

JEAN. No.

> *Pause.*
>
> ROY *throws* JEAN *a cigarette.*
>
> *Pause.*
>
> *He gets up, goes over to the bed, and lights her cigarette.*
>
> *He hovers about.*
>
> *The doorbell rings.*
>
> *Pause.*
>
> JEAN *gets up quickly, and goes out to answer the door.*
>
> ROY *sits in the armchair.*

DAWN *(off).* Ooh, blimey, Jean, never thought I'd bleedin' get 'ere. Bet you thought I worn't comin', dint ya?

JEAN (*off*). Yeah.

DAWN (*off*). . . . eh?

JEAN (*off*). Yeah.

DAWN (*off*). 'E ent been 'ome, 'as 'e?

JEAN (*off*). Ant 'e?

> *By now,* DAWN *is preceding* JEAN *into the kitchen.*

DAWN. 'E ent been 'ome, I'll bleedin' murder 'im when I get 'old of 'im, Jean.

> *She sees* ROY.

Ooh, fuck! (*Quietly.*) 'Oo's 'im?

JEAN (*quietly*). Go on.

DAWN (*quietly*). Eh?

JEAN (*quietly*). Go on in.

> DAWN *comes into the room proper, followed by* JEAN.

DAWN. 'Iya.

ROY. 'Ow d'yer do.

JEAN. This is Roy. This is Dawn. So, 'e 'ant been 'ome then?

> DAWN *gets out a cigarette.*

DAWN. 'As 'e fuck been 'ome, Jean, 'e ent. Went out dinner-time today, ent seen 'im since. Dint go to work, see? Couldn't get up – drinkin' till two a.m.

> ROY *lights* DAWN's *cigarette.*

DAWN. Oh, ta.

ROY. This your friend, then?

JEAN. Yeah.

DAWN. Gorreny money, Jean?

JEAN. Yeah.

DAWN. I'm short now, see? Twenty quid 'e give me, Jean, twenty quid to last me the week. Then 'e borrows 'alf on it back. Michelle ate a five-pound note.

JEAN. 'Er ate it?

DAWN. Well, I mean 'er dain't eat it, but 'er chewed it up into little bits. Could've shoved me bleedin' purse down 'er throat, I tell ya.

ROY. You got a babysitter, then?

DAWN. Eh?

ROY. You got a babysitter?

DAWN. Ooh, yes, thank you.

Pause.

Live upstairs, do ya?

ROY. No.

DAWN. Oh. Thought you might've done.

ROY. Well I don't.

DAWN. Oh.

Pause.

Where d'you live then?

ROY. Why?

DAWN. Eh?

ROY. Why?

DAWN. I'm asking, in' I?

ROY. Round the corner.

DAWN. Oh. Not far then.

ROY. No.

Pause.

JEAN. Think I'll put me shoes on.

She does so.

DAWN. Jesus, are you 'ot or summat?

JEAN. Eh?

DAWN. State of 'im, Jean.

JEAN. Oh.

DAWN. Froze, I am.

JEAN. 'Tis cold, init?

DAWN. 'Tis, init?

ROY. Come over by the fire, then.

DAWN. D'you mean?

ROY. 'T's warmer over 'ere.

DAWN. Ooh I'm alright 'ere, thank you.

ROY. Come on.

DAWN (*going*). Eh? (*As she passes in front of* ROY.) 'Scuse me.

JEAN. Why don't you sit 'ere, Dawn?

DAWN. Ooh, no, don't be so daft, Jean. I'm alright 'ere.

JEAN. Let Dawn sit there.

    Pause.

ROY (*getting up*). 'Ere y'are, come and sit 'ere.

DAWN. Oh. Thank you.

ROY. Want a drink, Dawn?

DAWN. Eh?

ROY. Wanna drink?

DAWN. Ooh ah, go on, I'll 'ave a little 'un – I don't want no gin,
though; can't abide it.

ROY. What about Martini?

DAWN. Oh ah, go on, I'll 'ave that.

    ROY *pours* DAWN's *drink.*

ROY. 'Ere y'are.

DAWN. Ta.

JEAN. I thought we were goin' out.

DAWN. We am – I'm ready when you am, I am, Jean.

JEAN. Oh, only I'm ready now, see.

DAWN. Yeah, right.

    JEAN *and* DAWN *start to get ready.*

ROY. You never said you was goin' out.

JEAN. Oh, well you never asked me.

The doorbell rings.

DAWN. Oo's that?

JEAN. I dunno. 'T'ain't for me, I know that.

JEAN goes out.

DAWN (*picking up* ROY's *shirt from the floor*). Yours, init?

VAL (*off*). Where is 'e? Eh?

Another door in the hall being rattled.

Eh?

VAL appears in the kitchen doorway.

ROY. What the fuck are you doin' 'ere?

VAL rushes at ROY, *pushing* DAWN *out of her way.*

VAL. You fuckin' bastard!

DAWN. Oh my God, what's goin' on?

VAL grabs ROY, *and they start struggling. Then they fall on the bed, and have a violent fight for some time. During this, probably before they actually fall on the bed,* VAL *drops her purse, unconsciously and not obviously.*

The following should be taken as an approximation of VAL's *utterances during the fight.*

VAL (*approximately*). You bastard. Fuckin' comin' round 'ere, I fuckin' knew it, all the time I'm stuck round there with them, you cunt, night after fuckin' night, 'ow long you think I – shit, you, I'll . . . you think you, think you can get away with it, do you? Think you can just, eh? Eh? Don't you? Eh? You cunt, you fuckin' shit cunt.

ROY. For fuck's sake!

The fight has continued, and at some point one end of the bed has collapsed. Finally, ROY *has pinned* VAL *down, and is gripping her throat.*

VAL. Geroff me, gerroff – bastard!

DAWN. 'Ey. 'Ey, 'ey, 'ey, come on, come on, gerroff! Geroff!

ROY (*to* DAWN). Fuck off!

VAL *is now on the floor, coughing.* ROY *gets to his feet.*

DAWN. All right. Leave 'er alone!

ROY *picks up the Martini bottle, and wields it weapon-like.*

DAWN. Don't be so fuckin' stupid – put that down!

ROY. You mind your own fuckin' business!

DAWN. Mind your bleedin' mouth!

ROY. D'you want one?

DAWN. Oh, ah? You and 'oo? You want to fight, go in the fuckin' street.

ROY. Bollocks!

VAL. Go on, then, use it! Go on, what're you waitin' for, eh?

VAL *gets up, and starts towards* ROY.

You spineless little wanker!

DAWN. Now, now, don't be silly!

VAL. Keep your nose out of this, you!

VAL *pushes* DAWN *against the partition.*

DAWN. Fuckin' ell!

VAL (*to* ROY). I'll 'ave you!

ROY. Oh, yeah?

VAL. I'll fuckin' 'ave you where it 'urts.

ROY. You what?

VAL. In your pocket. And don't you fuckin' dare come 'ome, neither, 'cos you're never going to see them kids as long as you live!

VAL *rushes out through the kitchen.*

ROY. Where the fuck are they?

VAL *rushes back, dislodging the 'Marley' door, which crashes to the floor.*

VAL. 'Where are they?' Where are they! What the fuck do you care where they are, eh?

ROY. Well, I didn't want 'em!

VAL. No, nor did I!

ROY. You fuckin' 'ad 'em, though, dint you?

VAL. Yeah, and you're goin' to fuckin' pay for them, Goldenballs!

She rushes out.

ROY. PISS OFF!

VAL *(off)*. UP YOURS! CUNT!

The front door slams.

Pause.

DAWN. Satisfied, am yer? You wanna watch where you'm bleedin' puttin' it, you do!

She goes out into the hall.

(off.) Jean! Jean . . .

ROY *puts down the bottle. Then he puts on his shirt, and does up the buttons. Then he takes a chocolate, throws the chocolate-box on the bed, grabs his cardigan, and walks out.*

The front door closes.

Pause.

DAWN *(off)*. 'Old on. 'Old on. 'E's gone, Jean.

JEAN *(off)*. Is it a mess in there?

DAWN *(off)*. 'E's bust yer bed, Jean. Tell ya now. Bust yer bed. Don't matter, though, Jean.

DAWN *and* JEAN *come into the room,* DAWN *leading the way.* JEAN *is crying.*

DAWN. Stupid bugger. Coming round, smashing other people's places. Jesus, Jean. *(She surveys the scene.)* You can't sleep on that, Jean. Can't! You'll 'ave to come up ours. Mick'll mend that for ya. 'Tain't no bother. Get 'im round tonight, 'tain't no bother Jean. Oh, blimey, Jean, where do you find 'em? Eh? Crawl out the bleedin' woodwork, they do.

JEAN. I go lookin' for 'em specially, you know!

DAWN. I know you do, you got a bloody gift for it, you 'ave!

JEAN. Oh ah, they're all 'and-picked. It's the first thing I say to 'em, 'You goin' to come round and smash the place up?' – If they say yes, it's alright.

DAWN. Ooh, don't.

JEAN. Ooh, God – I thought the bloody lot'd 'a' gone, y'know –

DAWN. Could 'ave.

JEAN. – The telly, the record player and everything.

DAWN. I know, could 'ave – did you 'ear 'im?

JEAN. Yeah.

DAWN. Jesus, Jean, 'er come in 'ere like a madwoman! Thought 'er was goin' to kill 'im, I did. Went for 'er with a bottle, an' all, y'know.

JEAN. Did 'e?

DAWN. Did! (*She indicates the floor.*) You'd 'ave 'ad a murder on your 'ands then, see?

JEAN. 'Ey: I bet 'er thought you was me, eh?

DAWN. Ooh, blimey, 'er scared me, Jean. Sent me flyin' a couple of times, you know. 'Er was waitin' outside, 'er was, when I come in.

JEAN. Was 'er?

DAWN. 'Er must've knowed 'e was 'ere.

JEAN. Mm.

DAWN. Must've knowed it, see?

JEAN. I'll tell you summat, I'm bloody glad you're 'ere.

DAWN. Ooh, ah.

JEAN. Look at this door out 'ere.

DAWN. Ooh ah, 'er's bust yer curtain.

JEAN. Let's stick it in the 'all, eh, prop it up in the 'all?

DAWN. Aye.

JEAN. 'Cos I've never used the thing, anyway.

DAWN. No.

The following whilst they carry the 'Marley' door out into the hall.

DAWN. Tell you one thing, Jean.

JEAN. What?

DAWN. There'll be no tea for 'im when 'e gets in tonight.

JEAN. Ho, no.

DAWN. Eh? Smacked botty, straight to bed.

They come back into the room.

JEAN. Huh . . . it ain't too bad, really, is it?

DAWN. Could've been worse, Jean.

JEAN. Ooh, ah.

DAWN. Could 'ave.

They look round the room. The following two lines of dialogue may be initiated by DAWN *or* JEAN, *depending on who in performance finds the purse first – which may vary from performance to performance, owing to the necessarily erratic nature of the moment when* VAL *drops the purse. However,* JEAN *is preferable.*

JEAN/DAWN. 'Ey, 'ere's your purse 'ere.

DAWN/JEAN. That ain't my purse.

Pause.

JEAN. Ooh blimey . . .

DAWN. Oh Jesus, it's 'ers!

JEAN *(taking out coins).* 'Ere – stick this in yer pocket, we'll 'ave a bloody drink out of it.

DAWN. Oh, Jean . . .

JEAN. 'Ere, there's a note 'ere, 'n' all. *(A pound note.)*

DAWN. Cor blimey, 't's 'er 'ousekeepin'!

JEAN. 'Ere, I'll chuck this up the 'all.

DAWN. No – don't put it up the 'all, put it on the step, they'll be on the bleedin' bell again, Jean.

JEAN. Ooh ah.

DAWN. Ah, you don't want that.

JEAN. Ooh, come on, let's get up that pub – I'm goin' to 'ave a bleedin' double when I get up there.

DAWN. Ooh ah. Knew 'e was a cunt, Jean. Knew it, soon as I caught 'is eyes, that's 'ow you see, you see. Can't blame 'er, Jean, can't. Married man, see? 'Tain't right. 'Tain't!

JEAN. Ey: d'you think they'll still be out there when we go out?

DAWN. Don't matter, Jean! 'Tain't your bother.

JEAN. Ooh, it ain't 'alf!

DAWN. Course it ain't.

JEAN. I'll 'ave to put me dark glasses on, I should.

DAWN. Blimey!

JEAN. 'Ey, Dawn . . .

DAWN. Yeah?

JEAN. Listen: if Mick's in the pub . . .

DAWN. Yeah?

JEAN. Don't tell 'im what 'appened, will yer?

DAWN. Course I wun't!

JEAN. I mean, not while I'm there – you can tell 'im tomorrow if you want, I just don't want to talk about it tonight, I don't want to mention it.

DAWN. Course I wun't! Won't tell 'im at all if you don't want me to, Jean, don't be so daft!

JEAN. Oh well, 't's up to you. I'll put the fire out. (*She does so.*)

DAWN (*going out*). You got everything, Jean?

JEAN. Yeah.

DAWN. Keys? Fags?

JEAN. Keys. Fags. Right.

DAWN. Don't forget that kitchen light, Jean.

JEAN. Right.

She puts out the lights, and they go out to the street . . .

DAWN (*off*). Ooh blimey, 't's nippy.

JEAN (*off*). Go and 'ave a look-round, see if it's all clear.

DAWN (*further away*). Don't be daft. There'll be nobody there.

JEAN (*in the distance*). Let's make a quick dash for it.

 Silence.

 Fade to blackout.

 End of Act One

ACT TWO

Night.

Lights up – darkness.

Then, from the street, and hardly audible –

JEAN. 'Ere it is.

LEN. Oh, aye.

 The front door is heard opening. Then –

LEN. Shall I leave this door, Jean?

JEAN. Yeah, you can leave that for 'em, Len – they know where I am.

 JEAN unlocks the door to her room.

JEAN. Just put this on the catch. Come on in then, Len.

LEN (*coming in*). Thank you. Nice little kitchen.

JEAN. Yeah.

LEN. Oh – it's a nice room, Jean.

JEAN. Oh, well it's alright, you know . . .

LEN. It's smashing.

JEAN. Well, it's big enough for me, any road.

LEN. See you got yourself a telly.

JEAN. Yeah.

LEN. Oh, I see – they've partitioned it off.

JEAN. Oh, ah, they just slung that in.

LEN. Well that's 'andy, in't it? (*Laughing.*) I see! You'd 'ave a job sleeping in that, wouldn't you?

JEAN. Yeah – I'd 'ave all the blood rush to me 'ead, wouldn't I?

LEN. Aye, you would, wouldn't you, aye?

JEAN. I think what must've 'appened, Len, is the threads've gone on them legs up there –

LEN. Oh ah.

JEAN. – 'Cos it's been wobbling about all over the place for ages, and it just went bump tonight.

LEN. Oh.

JEAN. Right. Well, I'll put you a record on.

LEN. Aye, that'd be nice.

DAWN (*in the street*). Don't ring the bell, Mick.

The bell rings.

LEN. 'Ere they are.

MICK (*in hall*). 'Ullo, 'ullo!

DAWN (*in hall*). Wake the bleedin' 'ouse up!

MICK (*banging the partition*). Anyone at home, like?

LEN. 'Ey-up, Mick!

MICK. Here you are – got the ole carry-out.

LEN. Aye. Aye.

MICK. Hope there's enough, like.

LEN. Aye!

MICK *and* LEN *indulge in a brief bout of playful mock-boxing.*

MICK. You big bollocks!

LEN. 'Ey-up! 'Ey! 'Ey!

DAWN. Wake the bleedin' dead, wouldn't 'e, Jean?

MICK. Right, Jean: couple o' glasses and we're away.

JEAN. Right.

DAWN. Eh? No, no, no, no, come on: before you start, get this bed mended first.

MICK. Oh, for Jesus' sake!

DAWN. Don't start, Mick: you said you'd do it!

MICK. Can we have a drink first, like?

DAWN. You 'ave any more to drink you won't be in no state to mend nothing!

MICK. Eh, anything for a quiet life.

(The following dialogue runs simultaneously with some of the preceding, and begins as MICK *is saying: 'Oh, for Jesus' sake'.)*

LEN. I'll be alright out the can, Jean, don't worry about me.

JEAN. I'll just give 'em a swill, Len.

LEN. Aye.

MICK. (*Eh, anything for a quiet life.*)
  Let's have a look at the bed; Jean, what's the problems with the old bed?

DAWN. 'M legs'm bust, in't they, Jean?

JEAN. Yeah.

MICK. Sorry, Dawn, I beg your pardon, 'tis Jean I'm talking to, 'tis her who knows.

DAWN. I'm tellin' you, en' I?

MICK. 'Tis her bed, she knows the problems – Jean?

JEAN. Well, I think the threads've gone on them legs up there, see?

DAWN. That's right.

MICK. Threads have gone on the legs, Len.

LEN. Aye. Aye.

MICK. Okay, we'll have a look at that, no problem.

LEN. Right-o.

  MICK *and* LEN *inspect the bed.*

MICK. Oh yeah, I see, yeah, yeah.

JEAN. Yes, best thing to do is to take these legs off 'ere, an' then we can 'ave it on the floor.

DAWN (*joining in with* JEAN). The floor, yeah, Mick, 'er wants these –

MICK. Ah, don't give me a pain in the ear.

DAWN. } I ent givin' you no pain in no ear.

MICK. } Grab the end of that there, Len.

LEN. Right-o, mate.

MICK. Throw it off here, like.

DAWN. Careful, careful!

MICK. Wait till I throw it – woa!

DAWN. Mind that fire!

MICK. Aw, for Jesus' sake, if you're not going to be any help, you can wait in the kitchen!

DAWN. Just tellin' you what 'er wants, 'en I?

MICK. Len – on its side, away from you.

LEN. Right-o mate: yonk it over!

They put the bed on its side; LEN *passes one of the bed-legs to* MICK.

LEN. 'Ere y'are, Mick.

MICK. Jesus, if you'd one like that, you could travel!

DAWN. 'Be rude!

LEN. No, this is completely split, you'll never get this leg in 'ere now, mate.

MICK. This hole here is bollocksed an' all, like.

DAWN. 'Course they am, 'er wants these'n's off, don't yer, Jean?

MICK. Ar, button it, will you?

DAWN. 'Tell me to button it!

MICK. Aye, there's been a weight on this bed.

DAWN (*quietly*). Shurrup, Mick, I've told you.

MICK. Kiss my arse.

DAWN. Oh ah.

(*The following dialogue runs simultaneously with the preceding, and begins after: '. . . a weight on this bed.'*)

LEN. Is that what you want, then, Jean? Shall we whip these legs off?

JEAN. I think that'd be best, Len.

LEN. Right-o, then, whip these off.

MICK. Whip these buggers off.

They remove the remaining good legs. MICK hands one to DAWN.

MICK. Here: stick that in your mouth.

LEN. 'Ere y'are, Dawn, can you 'old these?

DAWN. Yeah.

MICK. And again. Right – let's get it back there, Len.

LEN. Alright, boy.

MICK. Woa!

JEAN. That lovely, thanks.

DAWN. 'T's alright, enit, Jean?

JEAN. Oh ah.

LEN. There. Let's have a drink.

JEAN. Thanks very much.

> JEAN *and* DAWN *make the bed.*

JEAN. Don't worry about that, just cover it up.

DAWN. } No bother, Jean.
LEN. } What would you like, then, Jean?

JEAN. I'll have anything, Len.

MICK. Here, I have Jean's drink here. Jean: that's for you.

JEAN. Ooh, thanks very much.

MICK. Nice drop of Rin-Tin-Tin.

JEAN. Yeah.

LEN. Is that what you want, Jean?

JEAN. Ooh, I like a drop of gin, Len.

LEN. What would you like, Dawn?

DAWN. I'll 'ave a lager, please, Len.

LEN. Aye, right.

MICK. Here y'are, Missus, I have your drink here: that's for you.

DAWN. I don't want no vodka, Mick.

MICK. For fuck's sake, you've been drinking vodka all night.

DAWN. I know.

JEAN. We've got some tonic here, you know.

DAWN. Don't matter, Jean, don't want no vodka, thank you.

MICK. I bought that for you special, like.

DAWN. I told you not to, didn't I?

MICK. Ar, please yourself. Don't ask for it again – give her a lager, Len.

LEN. Is that what you want then, Dawn?

DAWN. Yes, please, Len – lovely.

LEN. 'Ere y'are, Dawn.

DAWN. Aw, lovely, 'kyou.

   JEAN *is in the kitchen*.

MICK. Don't suppose you've got an old rasher sandwich in there, Jean, eh?

JEAN. No, I int.

MICK. You haven't got a rasher?

JEAN. No.

MICK (*quietly to* DAWN). Fuck's sake, I thought you told me she'd have a rasher, like.

DAWN. Blimey, Mick, leave it alone, will ya?

JEAN. I got some bread, though.

MICK. Ah, no, you're okay, Jean, no. No problems – y'know.

DAWN. 'E's alright, Jean.

MICK (*quietly to* DAWN). I just thought there might be a fuckin' rasher in it.

DAWN (*quietly*). Aw, bleedin' stomach.

LEN. Nice place Jean's got 'ere, init?

DAWN. Too small for 'er, Len.

JEAN. It's alright, y'know.

LEN. Aye, it's small, but it's compact.

JEAN. Ah well, there ain't much to clean, that's what I like about it.

LEN. Aye, that's the main thing, intit?

DAWN. Tek me shoes off, Jean, 'scuse me.

LEN. Tek me jacket off, Dawn.

DAWN. Yeah – 'preciate the benefit, Len.

JEAN. Just stick that anywhere, Len.

LEN. Aye.

All four have now sat down.

LEN. Nice to see you all again, anyway.

JEAN. Yeah.

MICK. 'Tis fuckin' nice to see you an' all, boy.

LEN. Cheers, cheers!

DAWN. Lovely!

MICK. All the best!

LEN. Cheers, mate! Cheers, Jean!

JEAN. Cheers.

DAWN. Jean – bit of a shock for you, wor'n it, eh, Len?

LEN. It was a shock, it was a shock – that's why I didn't recognise you, Jean: I didn't expect to see you.

JEAN. No, I didn't expect to see you, either.

DAWN. 'Course yer didn't. Kept it secret, I did.

JEAN. Ah, you din' 'alf.

DAWN. I never said a word to 'er. Never said a word.

LEN. 'E never said a word to me.

MICK. No – there you are, you see, 'course, she would have it, Big-Mouth McSweeney would blow the whole bloody gaff, but – did I say a word to you, Len?

LEN. No, no – no – no – Dawn, Dawn –

DAWN. Yeah?

LEN. In all fairness to Mick, 'e dint say a word to me about it.

DAWN. Alright, alright, I believe you.

JEAN. 'Er never said nothing to me, either; 'er just said we'll go for a drink Friday night, so round 'er comes, up the pub we goes, and there you were. Weren' 'alf a shock!

LEN. Aye, a good'n, wo'n'tit?

DAWN. Jean, Jean: Tuesday night, 'e brings 'im 'ome; didn't know 'oo it was, Jean, did I? Didn't know 'oo it was.

MICK. No, I didn't know who it was, an' all on Tuesday night . . . I'm standing in the bar, taking my pint . . . (*He mimes a hand tapping on his shoulder*). 'Who the fuck is this?' like. Big smile all over his ugly old mug. 'I know that face. Fuckin' Hardwick!'

JEAN. You look ever so different, though, Len.

MICK. Ah, yeah, you've changed.

DAWN. No, 'e ain't changed!

LEN. Well, you get older, don't you?

DAWN. Only the glasses, Len.

MICK. We all get older, like.

LEN. Of course, you 'aven't seen me wi' glasses, 'ave you? – Well, that's the difference then, intit? Aye.

JEAN. Yeah.

DAWN. Been through it though, ent ya? Can tell, Len: see it in yer face.

LEN. Well, I've 'ad me ups and downs, but what with one thing and another, it evens itself out in the end, doesn't it?

JEAN. Yeah.

MICK. You're better off for it.

LEN. Yeah.

MICK. You're your own man – you can wake up in the morning, pack your bags, head off up the High Road, no bother on you.

LEN. Aye. Aye.

DAWN. Thanks very much, Mick: you know where the door is, don't you?

MICK. I wasn't fuckin' saying anything, like.

DAWN. You can see 'im bachelor gay, couldn't ya? Can't even boil an egg, you.

MICK. There's more to life than boiling eggs.

LEN. Now, now, Mick, I might be footloose and fancy free, but you're a lucky man, I'd give a lot to be in your shoes – you've got a nice flat, three lovely little girls – four lovely little girls with you, Dawn, if you don't mind me saying so.

DAWN. Ooh, blimey!

MICK. Aye, she's got a mouth on her you can hear at Marble Arch, like.

LEN. In some ways it's a surprise to see them two still together – d'you know what I mean, Jean?

JEAN. Ooh ah!

DAWN. Surprise to me, Len.

LEN. No, no, no, seriously, Dawn, we're 'avin' a joke now, but seriously, to see you two still together now, after all this time, so 'appy, and mekkin' something of your lives, well it warms my 'eart, and I just wanted to tell you that, anyway.

MICK (getting up). Put it there, Len baby – you're one of the best. Drink up, boy – go on.

JEAN. Yeah, let's 'ave a top-up.

DAWN. Ooh ah, Jean.

MICK. You were away a long while, but you weren't forgotten.

JEAN. 'Ere y'are.

DAWN. Ta, lovely, Jean.

LEN. I meant what I said, Mick, you know that, don't you?

MICK. I know that, Len-baby. From the heart. Aw Jesus, Jean, you've a snap here of the girls, eh?

LEN. Ooh, look, there they are, aye. Don't they look nice?

MICK. That's Tracy Dawn, like.

LEN. Oh, that's Tracy, is it?

MICK. Tracy.

DAWN. Tracy . . .

MICK. And that's Michelle, like.

LEN. Michelle – oh, doesn't she look lovely?

DAWN. Just about to start grizzling there, Len.

MICK. And that's my little favourite, Simone.

LEN. Simone, ah!

MICK. French name, like, you know . . .

   MICK *starts an asthma attack.*

LEN. Aye. What's up, Mick? You alright?

JEAN. 'T's 'is asthma.

DAWN. Come 'ere to me.

LEN. Oh, 'e still gets 'is asthma, does 'e?

JEAN. Yes.

LEN. Oh dear.

DAWN. That's what 'e gets from drinking till two in the morning, Len.

LEN. Like a blockage, is it?

DAWN. No, it's alright, 'e's got 'is spray.

   DAWN *pounds* MICK's *back.*

JEAN. They're nice kids, int they?

LEN. Aye, don't they look lovely?

JEAN. Mm . . . 'er's my favourite – Tracy.

LEN. Aye.

JEAN. 'Er's a character, 'er is.

LEN. Aye, got a cheeky little face, 'asn't she?

DAWN. Jean.

JEAN. Eh?

DAWN. Y'ain't got a packet o'soup, 'ave ya?

JEAN. Oh. I might 'ave.

DAWN. Eh? Only 't 'elps 'im, see, when 'e's like this.

MICK. 'Elps; you know . . .

JEAN (*suddenly remembering*). Ooh – I've got a tin of tomato soup.

DAWN. Lovely.

JEAN. D'you wannit now?

MICK. Jes', I wouldn't mind it now, Jean.

JEAN. Oh, alright.

DAWN. I'll mek it, Jean. I'll mek it.

JEAN. No, you sit yourself down.

DAWN. No bother.

JEAN. No, I'll just stick it on. Can I just come by 'ere, Len?

LEN. Sorry, Jean! Y'alright? There y'are.

JEAN. Oh, you didn't 'ave to move.

LEN. No, you're alright.

Pause. JEAN *organises soup, saucepan, etc.*

LEN. You alright in there, Jean? D'you want a 'and, like?

JEAN. No, I'm alright, Len, thanks.

LEN. 'Ave your drink with yer, anyway. 'Ere y'are, 'ere's your drink.

JEAN. Thanks.

DAWN. Len.

LEN. Aye?

DAWN. D'you wanna fag?

LEN. Aye – don't mind if I do, Dawn, thank you.

DAWN. Jean.

JEAN. Eh?

DAWN. Wanna fag?

JEAN. Alright.

DAWN. Tek 'er a fag, Len.

LEN. I'll light it for 'er. I'll light it for you, Jean.

JEAN. Thanks, Len.

LEN. 'Ere y'are, Jean: lit it for you.

JEAN. Thanks Len.

LEN. Where's your toilet, Jean, if you don't mind me asking?

JEAN. Go out of 'ere, turn left, it's just the door on your right.

LEN (*going*). Right. Thank you.

JEAN. There's a light switch just in front of you there; just push it.

LEN (*from hall*). Oh, ah, aye. Thank you.

DAWN. Alright, am yer?

MICK. I'm alright.

DAWN. Should've got you tomato soup for your breakfast – might've got you to work.

MICK. Nobody eats tomato soup for their breakfast.

DAWN. Jean.

JEAN. Eh?

DAWN. Jean: it's a shame, intit? Shame, for Len.

JEAN. Oh; yeah.

DAWN. 'Is wife ran off an' left 'im, Jean.

JEAN. Yeah. 'E's been telling me.

DAWN. Told yer, yeah. Run off with a salesman. Been 'urt, 'e 'as.

JEAN. Yes, well anybody would be, wouldn't they?

DAWN. Ooh, ah. You couldn't do it to 'im, could yer, eh? Couldn't do it to 'im. 'E's that sort, though, see, Jean, gets 'urt easy.

MICK. Very soft-hearted.

DAWN. Ooh, ah, don't carry no airs.

MICK. No airs or graces.

DAWN. What's 'e say to you, Mick?

MICK. Eh?

DAWN. What's 'e say to you?

MICK. 'E didn't say fuck all to me.

DAWN. Ooh, blimey! You don't tell me nothing, you.

MICK. No, I don't poke my nose in there, Jean.

JEAN. No.

MICK. You know what I mean: what's passed is passed, that's his own affair, like.

JEAN. 'Tis. Yeah.

DAWN. No, but 'er must've been a flighty bit, though, Jean.

JEAN. Well, you don't know – you can't tell, can yer?

MICK. Don't suppose you got an old sausage to go along with the soup, Jean?

JEAN. No, I got nothing like that.

DAWN. Blimey, 't ain't no caffy, Mick. Ent done nothing but go on about 'is bleedin' stomach since 'e left that pub, Jean.

MICK. I was only asking. Am I out of order? Jean knows me.

DAWN. Ooh, ah, 'er knows you alright.

MICK. If I'm out of order, Jean'll tell me I'm out.

DAWN. 'Not sayin' you'm out of order.

MICK. Jean: am I out of order?

JEAN. No, no.

MICK. There you are, you see. Jean knows me. I didn't eat all day.

DAWN. Ooh, blimey, Mick, me 'eart bleeds for you – d'you 'ave enough to drink?

MICK. I'll have a rasher sandwich when I go home.

DAWN. You'll 'ave no rasher sandwich, you won't touch that bacon, you'll 'ave egg.

MICK. Didn't I have two egg sandwiches already today?

DAWN. That bacon's for breakfast.

LEN *returns*.

DAWN. Alright, am yer, Len?

LEN. Aye, ah: better out than in.

JEAN. 'T's a weight off your mind, init?

LEN. Aye.

DAWN. Enjoyed yourself tonight, ant yer?

LEN. Aye.

DAWN. Ey? – enjoyed yourself.

LEN. It's been a grand night.

MICK. It's been a great night.

JEAN. Yeah, it's been a good night.

LEN. Aye . . . Cheers, anyway.

JEAN. ⎫ Cheers!

DAWN. ⎭ Cheers!

MICK. All the very best.

LEN. You know, come back to London, it's a big old place, and
after all this time, meeting up with you again, well, it's a bit
unexpected really, intit? But you know, although there are so
many people in London – well, there are thousands of 'em –
millions, really, aren't there? – although there are so many, if
you don't know anyone, it can be a bit lonely, to be quite
frank with you.

DAWN. Oh, it can be very lonely, Len.

LEN. Aye. So, bumpin' into you again, and 'avin' a drink and a
laugh, well it makes a big difference, and I do appreciate it,
and I just wanted to tell you that, anyway.

MICK (*getting up*). Put it there, Len-baby.

LEN. Uh, Mick!

MICK. There you are, you see: this man's from Corby, and I'm
from Cork, but we don't give a fuck. That was always our
motto: Have A Drink, And Don't Give A Fuck!

DAWN. 'E ain't from Corby, Mick.

LEN. It dunt matter, Dawn.

MICK. What're you talking about?

DAWN. I'm talking about Len: 'e ain't from Corby.

MICK. Where's he from, then? I know this fuckin' man for years, and I'm telling you he's from Corby. 'Len From Corby.'

DAWN. 'Be stupid.

MICK. Len, you're a Corby man, aren't you – Jesus, I'll give you a pound note on it. There y'are! Len: where are you from?

LEN. You just lost yourself a quid, Mick: I'm not from Corby.

DAWN. Told ya.

JEAN. From Lincolnshire.

MICK. Ar, for Jesus' sake, you always told me you were from Corby.

LEN. No; no, what it was, Mick, before I came to London the first time, I worked in Corby.

MICK (*pocketing the pound*). There you are, you see – he worked in Corby, what am I telling you?

DAWN. Nothing to do with it!

MICK. 'Have A Drink, And Don't Give A Fuck', mm? Ah, that was always the way with us, yourself and meself, into every pub on the Kilburn High Road. (*Continues whispering into* LEN's *ear.*)

LEN (*laughing*). Aye!

MICK. Wild fuckin' men! They'd see us comin' a mile away. More money than sense.

LEN. Were younger, then, of course, weren't we?

MICK. We were younger then, of course, you see? I've seen the time I could sit down to eighteen or twenty pints, no bother on me. That was the way with us: money on the counter, get the pints down you, and hump the fuckin' begrudgers!!

DAWN. Jean, d'you wanna fag?

JEAN. Mm.

DAWN. Do ya? Alright, am ya?

JEAN. Yeah. Yeah.

DAWN. I'm froze, y'know.

JEAN. D'you wanna sit 'ere?

DAWN. No, pass us me coat.

JEAN. 'Ere y'are.

DAWN. Lovely, ta.

(The following dialogue runs simultaneously with the preceding and carries on directly from: '. . . and hump the fuckin' begrudgers!!')

LEN. Then we'd go down the West End, occasionally, wouldn't we? Soho, down there.

MICK. Soho. Great place, the West End.

LEN. Aye.

MICK. I haven't been down there this years.

LEN. 'Aven't yer?

MICK. And then we'd roll home all hours of the fuckin' morning, like, back to the digs. Jean, we had this old digs up the road there, Mrs Clancy's –

JEAN. Yeah.

MICK. – We'd fall in the door four o'clock in the morning, pockets full of beer, 'Ssh-ssh!!' *(He bangs on the floor with his foot.)* 'If you boys don't keep quiet, you'll get no breakfast in the morning!'

LEN. Aye. Wonder what 'appened to 'er.

MICK. She's still up there.

LEN. Is she?

DAWN. Ooh, ah. 'E stayed with 'er, didn't you?

MICK. Oh, yeah: I stayed with her.

LEN. Did you?

MICK. Time Dawn's mother came down from Birmingham; time Michelle was born.

DAWN. Simone.

MICK. Was it Simone?

DAWN. 'Course it was Simone – Tennyson Road.

MICK. Oh, well. I stayed there for a couple of weeks, like. Very nice.

LEN. Mm.

MICK. Religious maniac.

LEN. Aye.

MICK. Off to Lourdes every five minutes, but very nice breakfast.

LEN. Aye, 't's a good a breakfast, I'll say that for 'er, did a good breakfast, aye.

Pause.

Wasn't she at your wedding?

MICK. Oh yeah. She was there.

LEN. Thought so.

MICK. Oh, Lord Jesus Christ, d'you remember the morning I got married?

DAWN. Ooh, blimey – don't!

MICK. Only for you giving me the big bumper of brandy to straighten meself out, I'd've never got anywhere near the church.

LEN. Aye, you were in a terrible state, Mick – you both were, you were an' all, Dawn. Jean, Jean, I'm surprised either of them can remember anything about that wedding-day, aren't you?

JEAN. Mm, yeah.

DAWN. Don't. Don't, Len – I don't remember me own wedding-day.

MICK. Jesus' sake, you must remember your wedding-day.

DAWN. No, Mick. Last thing I remember is them toilets in the Old Bell.

MICK. But you remember the church, like?

DAWN. 'Course I remember the church – I ain't on about the church!

MICK. That's all I'm saying, like – everybody remembers their wedding-day.

DAWN. It's the rest of it I don't remember.

MICK. I remember us standing around outside the church, waiting for the pubs to open. Big Eddie an' all the boys, hanging around.

LEN. We went round to Jean's, didn't we?

DAWN. 'Course we did, 'course we did!

MICK. Ah yeah, you're right, man – we went round to Jean's.

DAWN. Yeah.

LEN. You laid on a right good spread, as I remember, Jean.

DAWN. She did.

LEN. Sandwiches, didn't you?

DAWN. Champagne, 'er laid on for us.

JEAN (*getting up*). Well, it was alright, y'know. Bridged the gap, any road.

> JEAN *goes into the kitchen to check the soup, and having done so, stays in the kitchen listening.*

MICK. Wouldn't mind one of them sandwiches now.

DAWN. Ooh, blimey, Mick. Need a bleedin' man-'ole cover, you do.

LEN. 'T's 'ard to imagine now, intit?

DAWN. Eh?

LEN. Where was that room you 'ad, then, Jean?

DAWN. Smyrna?

LEN. Smyrna.

DAWN. Yeah.

MICK. Aw, Jes' – d'you remember us all standing round at

Smyrna? Aw, the room was smaller than this. All hunched up like sardines.

DAWN. Ah, it was lovely, though.

MICK. Aw, 'twas very nice, I'm not saying, Jean – it was very nice.

JEAN *returns, pours herself another drink, turns over the record, and sits down, whilst –*

LEN. Aye. Aye.

MICK. Then, all down the boozer soon as it opened, for a few pints.

DAWN. That was my mistake, that was.

MICK. You had to go to the pub, like. You had to put in an appearance.

DAWN. I know, but I went mad, Mick, I drunk meself stupid.

MICK. Ah well, like, you can't take it, like.

DAWN. Couldn't then, proper laid up.

LEN. Was you?

DAWN. I was – I couldn't get off me knees in them toilets. Couldn't lift me 'ead up.

MICK. I don't remember that.

DAWN. No, well you was pissed up an' all, worn't ya?

MICK. I was not pissed up, I was havin' a few jars on my wedding-day, like.

LEN. Then Jean 'ad to take you 'ome, didn't she?

JEAN. Yeah.

DAWN. She did, I was proper poorly, Len. Woke up in that room, Len, didn't know where I was. 'E worn't there, me own 'usband on me wedding-day.

MICK. I had one or two other calls to pay. Fellows wanting to shake my hands and buy me a drink – 'tis not every day you get married.

DAWN. 'Uh – start off as you mean to go on!

LEN. I was round there the other day.

DAWN. Where?

LEN. Messina.

DAWN. You worn't!

LEN. Aye, I was up that way, and I saw the 'ouse, and I
    wondered if you'd still be living there – I didn't think you
    would be, but I thought you might've left your address, like.

MICK. Haven't been round there this years, like.

LEN. No, no. I tapped on the window like we used to; black man
    came to the door.

DAWN. Oh, blacky living there, is there?

LEN. Yeah, big, 'e was, just in 'is trousers and vest – didn't seem
    to know anything about you.

DAWN. 'E wouldn't.

    Pause.

LEN. We had some good times round there, though, didn't we?

MICK. Uh . . . some great nights in Messina.

LEN. Few drinks, eh?

MICK. Round there with the carry-out.

LEN. Aye. 'Course, you two were there, weren't you? Then you
    moved out, and 'e moved in.

JEAN. That's right.

DAWN. Don't talk to me about Messina Avenue, Len; brought
    my first babby into the world in Messina Avenue, I did.

MICK. Tracy Dawn.

DAWN. Ooh, terrible.

LEN. You 'ad 'er there, did you?

DAWN. Ooh, no. I didn't 'ave 'er there, 'ad 'er up St Mary's,
    Paddington – where 'er 'ad 'ers, Princess Anne.

MICK. For Jesus' sake!

LEN. Oh? Oh, did you?

DAWN. We was livin' there, though, Len: one room.

MICK. We weren't there all that long, like.

DAWN. Long enough, Mick.

LEN. Must've been about six years ago, that, now, mustn't it?

DAWN. No.

LEN. Aye, six years.

DAWN. No, 'er's nearly eight, Tracy.

LEN. Eight?

DAWN. Yeah: 26th of January, 1972, 'er was born.

LEN. Eight years ago, is it? Doesn't seem like it, does it?

MICK. Time flies.

LEN. It does, mate, dunt it?

JEAN. You workin' tomorrow, then, Len?

LEN. No, no; the job I'm on, er, buildin' this synagogue up in 'Endon, so I don't work Saturdays.

JEAN. Oh.

MICK. Oh, yeah, the Jew-Boys, they have their Sunday on a Saturday.

LEN. Aye. Aye, that's right.

MICK. Is that a big job, Len?

LEN. No, no. It's not the synagogue itself, like, it's more like a church hall, an extension on the back, I should think it'd be about five weeks – six weeks at the most I should think, Mick.

MICK. You'll pick up another job at the end of that, no bother.

LEN. No trouble at all, no.

MICK. See, that's the way with us, Jean: we are not skilled men, but we're all-round men, like.

JEAN. Yeah.

MICK. We can walk onto the site there, we can say to the Ganger-Man, 'We can lay your cables, lay your pipes, we can do your tarmac, we can do your pavements, do your kerbs, do your concreting, di-da-di-da-di-da, like'.

LEN. You see, we're not skilled men, Jean, but we're experienced men.

JEAN. Yeah.

MICK. We work in shit. All weathers.

DAWN. Aooh, ah!!

LEN. See, that's why I come down to London, Jean; no end of building jobs going on down 'ere. Whereas, in other parts of the country – up north, for instance, not so much.

JEAN. No.

LEN. But down 'ere, as I say, if you're an experienced man, like Mick and myself, they're crying out for you – crying out.

MICK. Oh, yeah.

DAWN. Crying out for you this morning, worn't they, Mick?

MICK. They can cry out all they want: there's a bollocks up in that job, Len, I love to see him suffer.

DAWN. Proper poorly, worn't ya?

MICK. I was! I wasn't well, you know I wasn't!

LEN. D'you 'ave yer chest, did you?

MICK. Chest was at me, Len. Why would I go out on a morning like that with this chest? I'm not a fuckin' machine, like.

DAWN. The chest 'e gets of a Friday morning after being paid the Thursday night, you know what I mean, Len?

MICK. Oh, you know all about it, like – you don't have to suffer it.

DAWN. Oh, I suffer it.

MICK *has another asthma attack.*

DAWN. Want me to thump ya?

MICK. I'm alright.

DAWN. Bleedin' thump ya.

Pause.

Use too much of that spray, you do, Mick.

MICK. It's the only thing is any good for it. Don't suppose that old soup's ready, Jean?

JEAN. Will be in a minute.

DAWN. Poison, that spray is, you know, Jean. Uses too much of it. Gives 'im the shakes.

JEAN. Yeah.

Pause.

MICK. Why would I go out every day, Len? I can get the money when I want it.

DAWN. Shame it don't come my way.

MICK. What're you talkin' about? We went to Cork in the summer: hundred smackers in her hand.

DAWN. Still in me 'and when I come 'ome, Len.

MICK. That's not what I'm saying: you got the money.

LEN. Mick was telling me about your 'oliday in Cork, Dawn. Sounds as if you 'ad a nice time?

MICK. We'd a lovely time, Len.

DAWN. Punishment, Len: punishment.

MICK. What are you talking about?

DAWN. What's the use of a 'undred pound, Mick, when there's nowhere to bleedin' spend it?

MICK. Well, the kiddies had a lovely time to themselves.

DAWN. They was over-excited.

MICK. They were excited because they'd never been by the seaside before.

DAWN. They was excited because they couldn't get out the bleedin' caravan, raining all the time.

MICK. My arse.

DAWN. Nothing for 'em to do, Len: bored stiff, they was.

MICK *(undertone)*. Thanks very much.

DAWN. } *(undertone)*. 'D'you mean?

JEAN. } This is Dolly Parton, Len. *(She is referring to the record.)*

LEN. Aye, aye. She's good, int she? Me wife used to 'ave a few of 'ers.

MICK. Who's that?

JEAN. Dolly Parton.

MICK. Oh – very good.

LEN. She's got a nice personality, ant she?

JEAN. Yeah.

MICK. Nice voice, an' all.

JEAN. Yeah.

DAWN. Looks like a bleedin' man dressed up as a woman, 'er.

MICK. I'm sorry, Dawn; like, I beg your pardon, I'm sorry to contradict you here, like, but how can she look like a man when she's got diddies out to here?

DAWN. Well, Danny La Bleedin' Rue's got diddies out to there – you'd fancy 'im, you.

MICK. I'm not talking about Danny La Bleeding Rue, I'm talking about Dolly Parton, and she doesn't look like a man.

DAWN. 'Er ain't natural. Put a bit of Elvis on, Jean.

JEAN. Yeah.

LEN. Oh, you got Elvis, 'ave you?

JEAN. Yeah.

DAWN. Yeah, we bought it for 'er for 'er birthday.

JEAN. 'T's good.

DAWN. Yeah – 'Greatest 'Its'.

LEN. Shame about 'im dying, wasn't it?

JEAN. Yeah.

DAWN. Ooh – I loved 'im Elvis, I did – loved 'im.

JEAN. And me.

MICK. Funny the way they all die, those stars. You got Elvis . . . Jim Reeves.

LEN. Jim Reeves.

MICK. Buddy Holly.

JEAN. Mind you, they were killed, weren't they?

MICK. They were killed.

JEAN. Buddy 'Olly, 'e was only 26, y'know. 'S young, that, init?

LEN. Oh, aye.

DAWN. Ah, but 'e got too fat, though, Elvis: see the state of 'im before 'e died, Jean?

JEAN. It's the drugs, weren'it? Blew 'im up?

DAWN. I don't know, you know.

JEAN. Ooh, it was.

MICK. You would never've taken Elvis for a junkie.

DAWN. You wouldn't; 'e worn't no long-'air, Elvis.

LEN. 'E was ill, wa'n't 'e?

DAWN. 'E was, you know.

LEN. They wouldn't 'ave given 'im all them drugs if 'e 'ant been ill.

DAWN. 'Course they wouldn't. You know what I think, Len? I don't reckon 'e knowed about them drugs.

LEN. No.

JEAN. 'Course he knew about 'em – 'e'd got 'yperdermic needles and boxes of pills all over the place at 'ome.

DAWN. No – them was doctors' drugs, Jean!

JEAN. No, 'e was bribing the doctors to give 'im all them.

LEN. Oh, aye, but 'e didn't smoke pot and that, did 'e?

JEAN. Oh no, no – 'e'd left that be'ind a long time ago.

LEN. Ah, well, there y'are, you see, that's what I'm saying, 'e wasn't like the Rolling Stones and them, was 'e?

MICK. Oh, no, Elvis was more clean-livin' than what the Rolling Stones were.

LEN. ⎫ Aye.
DAWN. ⎬ Ooh ah.

JEAN. Ah, well, they've all got too much money anyway, int they? They don't know what to do with it.

DAWN. Oh ah, it's money kills 'em, Jean.

MICK. Ah, this is it: they can't take the strain. Like meself.

LEN. I know what you mean, Mick, I know what you mean – I don't know what to do with all my money.

DAWN. Don't you, Len?

LEN. I thought I might buy a yacht, or I might . . .

Short pause.

JEAN. I wouldn't like a lot of money, me.

LEN. Wouldn't you?

JEAN. Well, not that much, any road. You go and die and leave it, don't you?

LEN. Aye, you can't take it with you, can you?

JEAN. You can't.

MICK. You can hit it a bit of a kick before you go.

JEAN. ⎱ Mm.
DAWN. ⎰ Mm.

Pause.

MICK. What'd you do now, Len, if you had a million pounds?

LEN. ⎞ Ooh!
JEAN. ⎬ Oh!
DAWN. ⎠ Ooh, blimey!

DAWN. Tell you what I'd do.

JEAN. What?

DAWN. Get meself a full-time baby-minder, twenty-four hours a day.

MICK. What do you think I pay you for?

DAWN. I wouldn't need your twenty quid, would I, if I 'ad a million pounds.

LEN. I think I'd get meself a little boat, down by the sea, do a bit of fishing.

JEAN. You like fishing, don't you, Len?

LEN. I do, I do.

Pause.

What'd you do, then, Jean?

JEAN. Me? I'd go to America.

LEN. Would you?

JEAN. I'd love it.

LEN. You always wanted to do a bit of travelling, didn't you?

JEAN. Yeah, go abroad.

LEN. D'you ever go?

JEAN. No.

LEN. Didn't you?

JEAN. No.

LEN. Aah.

MICK. I have a sister in Chicago.

JEAN. ⎫ Mm.
LEN. ⎬ Oh?

DAWN. Ar, 'e 'as.

Pause.

LEN. What'd you do, then, Mick?

MICK. If I had a million pounds?

LEN. Aye.

MICK. I'd buy meself a pub.

DAWN. 'E would, 'n all, 'im.

MICK. I wouldn't bother opening it. I'd just sit in it meself.

JEAN. Well, you got a ready-maid barmaid anyway, ent ya?

DAWN. Blimey, Jean, you'd never be off your bleedin' feet, servin' 'im.

MICK. Don't worry yourself – big sign over the door: MEN ONLY, SELF-SERVICE.

DAWN. You could see it, couldn't you? Parlatic from morning till night.

MICK. And why the fuck not? Come on, this is supposed to be a party – come on, drink up there.

LEN. Right. Lager, Dawn?

DAWN. Yes, please, Len, lovely.

MICK. Your vodka is sittin' there.

DAWN. Ooh, don't want no vodka, Mick. Alright, go on, go on, go on, crack it open.

LEN. Don't you want a lager?

DAWN. Aye, I'll 'ave a lager an 'all.

LEN. Right.

JEAN puts the soup on the table.

MICK. There's my lovely soup coming.

DAWN. Lovely.

LEN. Spot of tonic in it, Dawn?

DAWN. Aye, throw it in there, Len.

MICK. Tell you what, Len-Baby, I'll sit there to take the ole loop-de-loop.

LEN. Eh? Oh, sorry Mick.

MICK and LEN change places.

LEN. Right mate? Right. Smells good, that soup.

JEAN. There's some bread 'ere.

DAWN. 'Ungry, am you, Len?

LEN. No, I 'ad my tea before I came out.

DAWN. Did ya?

LEN. Oh, yes.

DAWN. Yeah.

JEAN has sat down.

LEN. Sorry, Jean, I didn't get you yours – d'you want some gin, Jean?

DAWN (*taking cigarette*). Oh ah. Alright, am yer, Jean?

JEAN. Yeah, yeah.

DAWN. 'T's alright like this, the bed, enit?

JEAN. Oh ah, yeah, lovely. Er, cigarette, Len?

LEN. No, I've got one on, thank you, Jean.

MICK. This out of a tin, Jean?

JEAN. Oh, ah.

MICK. She always gets me it out of a packet, like, but this is very nice.

LEN. 'Ere y'are, Jean.

JEAN (*taking drink*). Thanks, Len.

DAWN. Alright am yer, Len?

LEN. Aye.

DAWN. Goin' to stay down 'ere now, am yer?

LEN. I might do; see 'ow it goes, like.

JEAN. See if you like it, eh?

LEN. Aye. If I like it, I might get meself sorted out and stop down 'ere, otherwise I might . . . go somewhere else.

DAWN. You don't miss 'er, do ya?

MICK. Ar, for Jesus' sake, give the man peace – you're like a dog with a bone. Pay no attention to her, Len – 'tis like goin' to fuckin' confession with her.

LEN. Aye, alright.

DAWN. You want to enjoy yourself, you do, Len. 'E's been through it, 'e 'as.

MICK. Well, if he didn't go through it before, he's going through it now!

DAWN. Looks well though, don't 'e, Jean?

JEAN. Yeah.

MICK. Looks fuckin' great.

LEN. Open air life – nothing like it.

DAWN. No 'e looks very well.

JEAN. I like you in them glasses, Len.

LEN. Huh . . . hide my face, don't they?

JEAN. No . . .

MICK. Hide the ugly old mug!

JEAN. No, I mean – they suit you.

LEN. Oh . . . cheers, anyway.

DAWN. } Cheers!
JEAN. } Cheers!

MICK. All the very best.

JEAN. 'Ave you done any fishing since you've been down 'ere, Len?

LEN. No, no, I left me rods up at me mother's like. If I decide to stop down 'ere, I daresay I'll go and pick 'em up, like.

DAWN. D'you eat them fish what you catch, do you, Len?

LEN. Some of them, aye. Some of the seafish make good eating.

DAWN. Do you?

LEN. Mm.

DAWN. Blimey.

JEAN. Lovely.

DAWN. Give us a taste o' that soup, Mick.

MICK. I will in my bollocks.

DAWN. Go on, I only want a taste.

MICK. This is my dinner. You had your dinner. Keep your nose out of my soup.

DAWN. Mean-'earted, you am.

MICK. Kiss my face.

DAWN. I'm goin' on the toilet, Jean.

JEAN. Alright.

> DAWN *has gone.*

> *Pause.*

JEAN. So d'you still get them 'eadaches, then, Len?

LEN. No, no, no I don't. The glasses seem to 'ave done the trick, aye.

JEAN. Ah, so it must've been starin' at the water strained your eyes.

LEN. Aye, watching the float, like, you see.

JEAN. Oh.

LEN. Anyway, as I say, I 'aven't 'ad a recurrence since I got 'em, so I put it down to that, aye.

JEAN. Good.

LEN. Ridiculous really, intit, goin' out for a day's fishing, and coming back with a 'eadache?

JEAN. Yeah – supposed to be enjoying yourself, ent ya?

LEN. Aye.

MICK. Thanks be to God I have no trouble with me eyes.

LEN. Aye, you're a lucky man there, Mick.

MICK. Ah well, we all have our little faults.

LEN. Aye.

MICK. You got your glasses; I got my chest; Dawn has her old mouth.

LEN. Ah, she's a good girl, Mick – you look after 'er.

> *Pause.*

> What's that you're reading there, then, Jean?

JEAN. This? That's Marilyn Monroe, but I've only read bits o' that.

LEN. Oh. Like 'er life-story, is it?

JEAN. Yeah, well – you know me: I always liked reading biographies.

LEN. Oh, aye, that's right, I remember, aye. I like novels meself. Harold Robbins, 'e's one of my favourites.

JEAN. Oh, yeah?

LEN. Ever read any of 'im?

JEAN. No.

LEN. Aye, very good stories, 'e writes. *Carpetbaggers* – that's one of 'is.

JEAN. Oh, I've read that.

LEN. That's it.

JEAN. Oh?

LEN. 'T's good, intit?

JEAN. Yeah.

MICK. Well, that was a fine drop of soup, Jean. Oh, that hit the spot.

JEAN. That's good.

MICK. I feel like a new man now. Jes's, I'm ready for a session now. Come on, Hardwick: drink up. I never saw you so slow.

LEN. Oh, don't you worry about me, mate – I'll keep up wi' you.

MICK. Jean – what about you?

JEAN. Oh, I'm alright, 'ere, Mick, thanks.

LEN. Jean, Jean, if you want to get to bed, like, just turn us out – don't let us overstay our welcome, like.

JEAN. No, don't be so silly.

MICK. Oh, for Jesus' sake, d'you know who you're talking to? This is Jean! This girl is a stayer – she'll drink us all under the table in no time. I'll say that for you, Jean: you could always take a drink. Oh, yeah, I've seen you in some sessions, hey? Drinkin' and singin' away to the small hours. D'you ever know about this girl, Len? – Lovely singer.

LEN. Oh, I'd forgotten that, Jean.

MICK. Aye, lovely voice –

LEN. – I remember, aye –

MICK. – Very sweet voice –

LEN. – Aye.

MICK. Oh, yeah. I love to hear her singin'. Tell you what, Jean.

JEAN. What?

MICK. I'll have one of your old songs off you before I go.

JEAN. Ooh, I dunno.

LEN. Aye, you'll 'ave to give us one, Jean.

MICK. Aye, yeah, Jean, lovely singer, ah yeah, you will – give us a song before I go.

JEAN. Can't remember 'em now.

MICK. Ar, Jean, pull the other one, 't 'as bells on. Go on, you'll give us one, won't you?

JEAN. I'll 'ave to 'ave another bottle o' gin first.

MICK. There's no problems with the old gin, Jean. Huh. Am I right?

LEN. Aye.

DAWN *returns.*

MICK. Am n' I right?

DAWN. 'Speak to me!

MICK. Ar, come near me.

MICK *draws* DAWN *to him, and she sits on his lap.*

DAWN. You've been mean to me, you 'ave.

MICK. Ar, give us an ole smile, it's supposed to be a party. I'm only sayin' to Jean here, we'll have a song off her before we go.

DAWN. Ar, only if 'er wants to.

MICK. Oh, I wouldn't twist her arm, like.

LEN. No no.

MICK (*to* DAWN). Come on, you! Drink up – enjoy yourself.

DAWN. } Cheers!

LEN. } Cheers!

JEAN. } Cheers!

MICK. All the Hairy Breast!

DAWN. 'Be rude!

MICK. Jean –

JEAN. Yeah?

MICK. It's very nice for me to be takin' a drink in your house.

JEAN. Ooh yeah, yeah.

MICK. Like, I only live around the corner, but we sort o' way lost touch, yourself and meself, over the last little while.

JEAN. Yeah.

MICK. And I'm sorry for it, and we won't let it be so long again.

JEAN. No, we wunt.

MICK. Okay.

JEAN. Yeah.

MICK. And, Jean –

JEAN. Yeah?

MICK. I'll have an ole song off you before I go.

JEAN. Oh!

DAWN. Cheers!

LEN. Cheers!

JEAN. Cheers!

DAWN. 'Ey, Jean, 'ave a bit of Elvis on.

LEN. Aye.

DAWN. Ain't 'ad 'im on yet.

JEAN. Let's 'ave a bit of 'im on.

> (*She starts putting on the record: Elvis Presley,* 40 Greatest Hits, *Record One, side one, 'My Baby Left Me'.*)

MICK. We'll have Elvis first, and then we'll have Jean.

JEAN. Then we'll show 'im up, eh?

MICK. Aw, Jesus, I had some drinks today.

DAWN. Ooh, blimey, you don't say.

MICK. I'm worn out picking winners.

LEN. Aye, you 'ad a lucky day, didn't you?

MICK. Yeah, I picked myself a nice little winner at Lingfield.
Then I met Sullivan, and I took some money off him at the
cards.

DAWN. 'Ow much d'you win off 'im?

MICK. Enough, like. I didn't take it all off him – I didn't want to
leave him short, like, you know.

DAWN. I never win nothing, I don't.

MICK. Ah, well, don't worry yourself, you've got a good-looking
husband.

DAWN. Ooh blimey, 'ark at 'im!

The music starts.

MICK. Elvis. The King.

JEAN. Yeah.

MICK. D'you ever go to an ole dance at all, Len?

LEN. Oh, we used to go a bit – occasionally, like.

DAWN. 'E does, don't ya?

MICK. Oh yes, I still go up to the 'National'.

LEN. Aye?

MICK. Or the 'Galtimore'.

LEN. Oh aye.

MICK. Dance all the way to the bar.

DAWN. Ooh ah.

MICK. She won't come with me.

DAWN. I bleedin' wunt – not after the last time I went wi' ya.

MICK. Oh, that's the way with me – dance all the way to the bar, like. Then dance all the way to the toilet. Then dance all the way back to the bar.

LEN. Aye. Aye. Know what you mean, mate.

JEAN. I ain't been to a dance for ages.

LEN. No, I an't, Jean.

DAWN. Ain't ya, Len?

LEN. No, we used to go a bit on 'oliday, like, at Skeg', but that'd be more discos, that's for the kids really, intit?

JEAN. Makes you feel old, dunnit, Len?

LEN. It does, dunt it?

MICK. I could never be bothered with a disco; I'd rather have a live band – like a show band.

LEN. Aye. Aye.

JEAN. We used to go a lot, dint we?

DAWN. Ooh, we did. We used to dance together, me'n 'er.

LEN. Did you?

JEAN. Ooh, ah, I loved it.

DAWN. Ooh, I did, Jean.

LEN. What they do that for, then?

DAWN. Eh? – Safer, Len.

JEAN. Ooh, ah! – What's safe about it?

DAWN. Ooh ah, I know, you could get some rough buggers down them places, you could see 'em coming across the floor towards you, and you knew.

JEAN. Ah, well, that's what we used to do it for, init?

DAWN. Ooh, ah – cattle market.

MICK *makes cattle noises.*

Eh? Ooh, don't be silly. I used to get dead sick, though, I did, Jean: always got the bleedin' ugly ones.

MICK. Thanks very much.

DAWN. Oh, no, it was different wi' you, Mick – took pity on you! No, we used to love the dancing, didn't we, Jean?

JEAN. Ooh, ah.

DAWN. We used to dance up the caff. Remember? The Coppola Arch?

JEAN. Coppola Arch!

DAWN. We used to be on them bleedin' tables, some nights.

JEAN. And that was just on a Coca-Cola.

DAWN. Oh, we didn't need no drink in them days, Len. D'you remember Kevin?

JEAN. Ooh, ah.

DAWN. 'E was a good dancer, worn'e? Bought me eternity ring, 'e did.

JEAN. Ooh, ah, I remember that.

DAWN. Yeah. Could be a cunt, though.

> LEN *starts to join in quietly with Elvis, tapping his foot to the music. Then* MICK *joins in, also quietly. The girls carry on over this, not noticing it yet.*

DAWN. 'Ey, what wa that little un's name, Jean?

JEAN. Which one?

DAWN. You know . . . 'e was only little, only 'ad a little bike, never 'ad a girlfriend, used to dance with a chair?

JEAN. Colin.

DAWN. Colin!

JEAN. Colin and Jeff – they were two brothers, Colin and Jeff. I used to dance with 'im sometimes.

DAWN. Ah – you was doin' 'im a favour though, worn't ya?

JEAN. Well, I felt sorry for 'im.

DAWN *(indicating the boys)*. Jean!

JEAN. Yeah.

LEN/MICK. 'Since my baby left me,
I found a new place to dwell

> Down at the bottom of Lonely Street,
> The Heartbreak Hotel.
> I'm feeling so lonely,
> I'm feeling so lonely, baby,
> I'm feeling so lonely,
> I could die . . .'

DAWN. Len.

LEN. Yeah?

DAWN. 'Tain't upsetting you, is it?

LEN. No, no, don't worry about me!

DAWN. Know you can feel free, don't ya – you'm among friends, don't you 'old it in.

MICK. Ah, footloose and fancy free.

DAWN. Ah, but a sad song, see? Can upset a person.

MICK (*loudly, and imitating Elvis*). 'Since ma baby left me . . .' (*etc.*)

JEAN. Ooh, en 'e good?

> MICK *continues imitation.*

JEAN. Sounds just like 'im, dunt 'e?

LEN. Aye, dunt 'e?

MICK. Oh, I could always do Elvis. You know.

DAWN. Jean! Jean: two of us on the backs o' them bikes!

JEAN. I know. It was dangerous, really, wunnit?

DAWN. Ooh!

JEAN. 'Cos we dain't wear no 'elmets, you know, 'cos you din' 'ave to, then . . .

LEN. No, you wouldn't . . .

JEAN. – It was just our bare 'eads.

DAWN. Remember that accident?

JEAN. Tommy!

DAWN. Ooh – on the way to Stourport, come off.

JEAN. Wa'n' 'e a mess, ey?

DAWN. Broke 'is arm.

MICK. We've seen some accidents. Eh, Len?

LEN. Ah.

JEAN. 'Ey: what about the day they all got picked up?

DAWN. The lads? Ooh, ah. 'Er went up the bleedin' Police
    Station, 'er did – layin' down the law to the coppers, 'er was!

JEAN. Nearly got meself put inside!

MICK. Pair of criminals, these two, Len!

LEN. Aye, Jean, Jean: wasn't it you 'oo told me about –

JEAN. Yeah, yeah – this is it –

LEN. – Mods and Rockers?

JEAN. – Yeah . . .

DAWN. Margate!

LEN. Oh.

JEAN. There was a great big fight, see, an' they all got arrested.

LEN. Oh, aye?

MICK. Pair o' Rockers, these two, Len.

JEAN. Oh, ah: we used to do ton-ups down the M1 'an't we?

DAWN. Yeah – silly, Jean!

    Pause.

JEAN. D'you remember that really bad fight with Tommy and
    . . . er . . . Den?

    Short pause.

DAWN. No.

JEAN. No – it was Colin.

DAWN. Ooh ah – wi' knives!

JEAN. 'E just touched Den's bike, an' 'e din' 'alf lay into 'im, din'
    'e?

DAWN. Abergelly.

JEAN. That's it!

MICK. We've seen some fights, eh, Len?

LEN. Oh, aye. Were they older than you, these boys, then, Jean?

JEAN. } Ooh, ah.
DAWN. } Ooh, ah – we was only kids, Len.

Pause.

JEAN. You used to 'ave a bike, din' you, Len?

LEN. Ah, when I was a lad, like, aye.

DAWN. Was yer a leather boy, was yer, Len?

LEN. For a year or so, like, aye.

JEAN. What was it?

LEN. A B.S.A.

JEAN. Oh, a Beezer. We didn't 'ave any o' them, did we?

DAWN. No.

LEN. No, this was an old bike – ten or fifteen year old when I 'ad it.

JEAN. They were all Nortons and Triumphs, wun' they?

DAWN. Yeah – Bonnyvilles.

LEN. Oh, no, no, no – I wasn't part of a gang, like.

DAWN. You 'ave a little girlfriend for the back, did ya?

LEN. From time to time, like. I got rid of it though.

DAWN. Did ya? Why?

LEN. I couldn't stand the cold, to be quite frank with you.

DAWN. Ooh!

JEAN. Bitter, wa'n' it?

DAWN. Ooh, could be very chilly – I used to get that cystitis, I did – on the toilet all the time, stinging, y'know.

MICK. How did you get that?

DAWN. Wind blowin' up yer skirt.

MICK. Oh-Ooh!

He puts his hand up DAWN's skirt.

DAWN (*laughing*). 'Ey – 'be rude!

JEAN. I bet we didn't 'alf look a sight, ey, on the backs of them bikes in them short skirts!

LEN. Mini-skirts.

MICK. I don't know, now, Len – I think the pair o'them have got very nice sets o'legs.

LEN. Oh, aye, aye, they 'ave, aye.

MICK. Jes', I don't know, this one has got shins so sharp you could shear a hedge with them.

DAWN. 'Be rude.

MICK. I'm only joking.

DAWN. Always goin' on about my body, you am.

MICK. You can't take a joke.

DAWN. Can.

MICK. Think you've got a very nice body. Kept your figure well. Jean – she's kept herself in trim, like.

JEAN. Yeah, yeah.

MICK. Know what I mean, Len like? Even though I do say it myself. She doesn't look like the mother of three kiddies.

JEAN *gets up, quickly and unobtrusively, pours herself a drink, and then stays up and at the drinks, facing away from the others.*

LEN (*continuing directly*). No, no: you've kept yourself very well, Dawn, no doubt about it.

MICK. That's what I'm saying, like. Oh, Lord Jesus, some of the ones, you see them on the Kilburn High Road, they have let themselves go, like; three or four kiddies in the pram, piled high with shopping bags, aw, Lord Jes', 'twould turn your stomach.

LEN. Aye.

MICK. Some of them are twenty-five, and they look forty-five, all fat and flabby, holes in their stockings. 'Twould make you wonder what they think of themselves.

LEN. Aye.

MICK. And their blokes, like. Some of the young ones, like, I see them when I'm up at the Dance, seventeen or eighteen years old, they got all the latest fashions, showing off their bodies, throwing themselves around the floor, making up to the geezers.

LEN. Aye.

MICK. But what are they? They're fuck all!

LEN. Aye.

MICK. There's nothing to them, Jean, you know.

JEAN. Mm.

MICK. But this one . . . this one is different.

LEN. Mm.

MICK. Dawn is a woman.

LEN. Aye.

DAWN. Eh?

MICK. Well, like, there's more to you than that, like.

DAWN. Oh.

MICK. I mean it now, I'm not bullshitt'n'. If you came up to the Dance with me, you'd show some of them young ones up.

DAWN. 'Be silly.

MICK. Jes', I don't know why you wouldn't bother coming up with me, like.

DAWN. You know.

MICK. Come up and give me an ole dance now and again.

DAWN. Goin' no Dances wi' you.

MICK. Come on, gimme a dance now.

He picks her up, and throws her about.

DAWN (*basically amused*). Don't be silly!

MICK. Oh, yeah!

DAWN. No, Mick!

MICK. Come on!

DAWN. No! Oh, geroff!

MICK. Hey, hey!

DAWN. Don't, you'll throw me back out.

MICK. Come on now!

DAWN. Careful, you'll have me throwing up.

> MICK *puts* DAWN *down.* JEAN *sits.*

LEN. I thought 'e were going to drop you then, Dawn.

DAWN. I know – 'e would, an' all, 'im. Rough bugger.

> *Pause: Elvis has begun, 'Love Me Tender'. The pause continues:*
> MICK *and* DAWN *cuddle up, then a few affectionate kisses, then a*
> *prolonged kiss. Then, quietly . . .*

DAWN. Let's 'ave a dance.

MICK. Oh, all of a sudden you want to dance.

DAWN. Oh, this is different.

MICK. I'm half-cut.

DAWN. I know, I am, an' all. Come on – don't matter.

> MICK *and* DAWN *get up and dance.*

> *After a short time,* MICK *taps* LEN *with his foot, and winks,*
> *gesturing him to dance with* JEAN.

> JEAN *immediately gets up and leaves the room.*

> *Pause. Elvis continues.* MICK *and* DAWN *continue to dance. Then*
> . . .

DAWN. Lovely to see you together, Len. You was fond of 'er,
worn't yer?

LEN. Oh, we always got on well, me an' Jean, aye.

DAWN. Get 'er to 'ave a dance wi' you, Len.

LEN. No . . .

MICK. Ar, go on, man – have a dance.

> LEN *laughs.*

> *As the track ends,* MICK *and* DAWN *have a prolonged kiss.*

> *The next track starts, 'Got A Lot of Livin' To Do', and* MICK *thrusts*
> DAWN *into a fast jive.*

MICK. Oh, that's more like it!

DAWN. No! I don't wanna do no rough dancing!

MICK. That's the kind I like.

They fall on the bed.

MICK. How did that happen?

DAWN. Aargh! Don't start gerrin' sexy! – 'Ey!

JEAN *returns.*

DAWN. Alright, am ya, Jean?

JEAN. Yeah, Yeah. 'Ow's everybody's glasses? Alright?

LEN. Aye, aye – come on!

MICK. Oh, I wouldn't mind an old jar.

JEAN. Len.

LEN. D'you want some tonic in that, Dawn?

DAWN. Ooh, ah.

JEAN. Mick.

MICK. Thanks very much, Jean.

LEN. 'Ere y'are.

MICK. I'll 'ave a drop of that vodka.

DAWN. You'll be sick, you will, Mick.

LEN. Want some tonic in there, Jean?

JEAN. Yes please, Len.

LEN. Say when.

JEAN. Right, that's lovely, thanks – don't wanna drown it.

LEN. No. (*Offering a cigarette.*) 'Ere y'are, Jean.

JEAN. Thanks, Len.

LEN. Dawn?

MICK. Here, I'll light that for her.

DAWN. Don't you inhale it, Mick.

MICK. No problems.

DAWN. You dare!

LEN. Dunt look right you with a fag in your mouth, mate.

DAWN. It don't.

LEN. Jean.

JEAN. I done it, Len, thanks.

LEN. Oh, aye – you're alright.

MICK. Come on, Jean – get the old record out of the way, and let's have a proper singsong.

JEAN. Oh, ah. That sounds more like it.

LEN. Oh, aye, let's 'ave a singsong, aye.

MICK (*withholding* DAWN's *cigarette*). What do I get for it?

DAWN. Oh, ah.

> DAWN *kisses* MICK. *He gives her the cigarette. He gets up.* JEAN *is seeing to the record.*

JEAN. Right . . .

MICK. Aw, here, I have to go to the toilet.

JEAN. Oh.

MICK. I have a loaded weapon. Jean, don't start without me.

JEAN. No – can't start without you; you know all the songs.

> DAWN *is also crossing the room.*

LEN. Are you going with 'im, Dawn?

DAWN. No – goin' to gerra drink o' water.

JEAN. There's a cup up there.

DAWN (*from kitchen*). Oh ar, I gorrit, Jean.

LEN. 'Ow much d'you pay for this room, if you don't mind me asking, Jean?

JEAN. Nineteen a week.

LEN. Nineteen pounds a week?

DAWN. Terrible, init, Len?

JEAN. Expensive, init? Eh?

LEN. Shocking.

JEAN. You thinkin' of moving out of your digs, then, Len?

LEN. Well, if I decide to stop down 'ere I'm thinking I might, but
 . . . nineteen pounds a week! Terrible price to pay!

JEAN. Well, that's 'ow much they cost now, see? 'Cos of course
 there int many about, so they just charge what they like.

LEN. Oh. But that other place you 'ad, er –

JEAN. Smyrna Road?

LEN. Smyrna Road, 'ow much was that?

JEAN. Oh, that was only eight.

LEN. Eight?

JEAN. But of course, that was a few years ago now.

LEN. Oh, aye, but eight to nineteen, that's er, that's – oo – that's
 over a 'undred per cent inflation – rocketing inflation, that is.

DAWN. Mmm.

JEAN. Well, you ain't gonna get anywhere like Messina Avenue, I
 mean that was only a fiver – well, it was four pounds,
 nineteen and six.

DAWN (in unison). – nineteen and six. For the two of us, mind,
 Len. Only one bed, though, Jean.

JEAN. Oh, ah, but it was still only one room, wunnit?

DAWN. Ah. (Pause.) Did 'er keep you waitin' again today, that
 woman?

JEAN. } Ooh, bloody 'ell!

DAWN. } Did 'er?

JEAN. Yeah. See, Len, the bloke 'oo owns these 'ouses, 'e owns a
 dress-shop on the 'Igh Road, see? An' I 'ave to go up there
 after work of a Friday, pay the rent.

DAWN. 'T's 'is wife, enit, Jean?

JEAN. Yeah. D'you know, I got in there today, an 'er'd got a girl
 in the back room, 'er was givin' 'er a fittin' for a wedding
 dress, so of course I was 'anging about for about twenty
 minutes.

LEN. No.

JEAN. I 'ave to wait, see, Len, 'cos 'er 'as to check me money and then write it in the rent-book, see?

LEN. No, no.

DAWN. Bleedin' cheek, enit, Len?

LEN. Terrible, ent it?

DAWN. Treat you like muck.

MICK *returns.*

MICK. Right, that's my throat cleared. Come on, Missus, sit down: we're going to start the singsong.

LEN. Aye, come on, let's get t'singsong going, then.

MICK. Come on, Jean – you get us kicked off.

LEN. Go on, Jean!

JEAN. Ooh, come on! You're the one that knows all the songs.

MICK. Ah, no Jean – you're the singer, come on now.

LEN. Come on, Jean!

JEAN. Ooh, I can't remember 'em now.

MICK. Aw, Dawn – what were the songs she used to sing?

DAWN. Ooh, I can't remember the names of 'em Mick?

MICK. Aw Jes' Christ, Jes', you had dozens of 'em, Jean.

JEAN *(sings).* 'Oh Danny Boy, the pipes,
          The pipes are calling . . .'
     Come on, you all know this one.

LEN *joins in, flat, and tagging behind* JEAN.

JEAN/LEN. 'From Glen to Glen,
          And round the mountain side.'

MICK. One voice: one singer, one song!

LEN. Sorry, mate, you're right, aye.

JEAN *(not having stopped).* 'The summer's gone,
     And all the leaves are dying.
     'Tis you, 'tis you are gone,
     And I must bide.

But come ye back
When summer's in the meadow,
Or when the valley's hushed,
And white with snow –

MICK (*harmonising*). And white with snow.

JEAN. 'Tis I'll be here
In sunshine er in shadow,
Oh, Danny Boy,
Oh, Danny Boy,
I love you so.' There y'are.

DAWN. } Oooh.

LEN. } Aaah.

MICK. Ah, Jean; from the heart: that was magic.

MICK *kisses* JEAN.

DAWN. Ooh, blimey! That's got to 'im, Jean.

MICK. Ah, that song gets me.

LEN. You've got a lovely voice, Jean.

JEAN. Ooh, gerrawf!

LEN. She's got a much better voice than some of them you get on telly, an't she?

MICK. Ar, the telly's all crap!

LEN. You ought to tek it up, Jean.

JEAN. Ooh, ah! (*To* MICK.) Come on, you do one now.

LEN. Come on, Mick.

MICK. Oh, no: I wouldn't follow that.

LEN. Ah, come on, mate.

JEAN. Len, come on: you do one!

MICK. Yeah, come on Len – your turn.

LEN. Oh, no!

DAWN. You used to know lots, you did, Len.

LEN. I only know t'dirty-uns we used to sing in the pub, like.

JEAN. Do one o'them.

MICK. Len, Len: give us one of your old Corby ones!

LEN. I don't know as I can remember 'em, er . . . oh, yeah. Er
    . . . Yeah . . .

He sings . . .

    'I knew a farmer, and I knew 'im well.
    I knew 'is daughter, and 'er name was Nell.
    She was so pretty, and only sixteen,
    And I showed 'er the works
    Of my threshing-machine.'

DAWN. Ooh!

JEAN joins in the chorus.

LEN/JEAN. 'I 'ad 'er, I 'ad 'er, I 'ad 'er, I 'av.
    I 'ad 'er, I 'ad 'er, I showed 'er the way.
    They were the best days of my life,
    I would say,
    And I spent 'em a-leading
    Young maidens a-stray.'

LEN (*solo*). I went to the farm, I took 'er one day,
    I took 'er inside,
    An' I showed 'er the 'ay.
    And under the 'ay,
    Where we could not be seen,
    I showed 'er the works
    Of my threshing-machine.'

MICK. You dirty bollocks!

LEN and JEAN sing the chorus. MICK claps.

LEN (*solo*). 'Now, three months later
    Could plainly be seen
    A bulge in 'er pinny
    Where no bulge 'ad been.
    And three months later
    Could plainly be seen
    The result of 'er playin'
    Wi' my threshing-machine.'

*LEN and JEAN sing the chorus. MICK does the odd whoop, in the
Country and Western style.*

LEN (*solo*). 'Now, three months later,
    The baby was born,
    The baby was born
    On a bright summer's morn.
    And between 'is legs
    Could plainly be seen
    A brand – new twin-cylinder
    Threshing-machine.'

DAWN. Oooh . . . dirty!

> LEN *and* JEAN *sing the chorus, then* . . .

LEN. I can't remember any more.

JEAN. Ooh, it's good, that one, Len.

DAWN. Didn't know you knew songs like that, Len. Dark 'orse, 'e
    is. Jean –

JEAN. Eh?

DAWN. Jean – what was tharrun?

JEAN. What?

DAWN (*sings*). 'I stood on the bridge at midnight . . .'

JEAN. Ooh, yeah – no, no, . . .
    (*Sings*.) 'It's the same the whole world over,
    It's the poor what gets the blame,
    It's the rich what gets the pleasure,
    Ain't it all a blooming shame?'

DAWN (*singing in unison*). '. . . Fucking shame?'

MICK. Hey, you, watch your language!

JEAN (*sings solo*). 'She was poor, but she was honest . . .'

> *Pause.*

JEAN. } Ooh!
DAWN. } Oooh, blimey . . .

> *Pause.*

JEAN/DAWN. 'She was poor, but she was honest . . .'

DAWN. Was about some rich geezer did it on 'er, wor'n it?

JEAN. Yeah.

MICK. Ah, Jean, give us another old Irish one, like.

JEAN. Ooh, you're the one that knows all the Irish ones.

LEN. Aye, Mick, come on.

MICK. Aw, no.

DAWN. No, 'e ain't got a note in 'is 'ead.

MICK. Fuck off! I could've sung in show bands!

JEAN. 'Ey, Len: you'd know this one. The only bit I know, is it
goes,
'Ta-rum, titty-bum, titty-bum, titty-bum.'

LEN/JEAN (*joining in*). 'Ta-rum, titty-bum, titty-bum, titty-bum.'

JEAN. That's the one.

> LEN *and* JEAN *continue to sing* 'Ta-rum', *etc., during which*
> DAWN *sings quietly to herself,*

DAWN. 'Roll me over,
In the clover,
Roll me over,
Lay me down,
And do it again . . .'

LEN (*to* JEAN). I know it – 'Ta-rum, titty-bum, titty-bum, titty-
bum –'

MICK. Ah, ta-rum titty fuckin' bum!

LEN. I can't remember it, Jean, it's gone.

JEAN (*sings*). 'When I was young,
I used to be
As fine a lad
As ever you'd see,
And the Prince o' Wales,
He said to me,
"Come and join
The British Army!" '

> MICK *joins in with the chorus* . . .

JEAN/MICK. 'Too-ra-loo-ra-loo-ra-loo,
They're looking for monkies
Up in the zoo,
And if I had a face like you,
I'd join the British Army!'

JEAN. That's good, init?

LEN. Oh. Come on, Jean – come on.

MICK. Don't stop now, Jean.

JEAN. Oh, I can't remember the other verses.

MICK. Oh, I love that one.

JEAN. Yeah; an' me, but they go out yer 'ead, dun't they? Come on, you do one, now.

LEN. Come on, Mick – your turn now. Come on, mate.

MICK. Ar, no, I won't bother.

LEN. ⎫ Oh, come on, Mick.

DAWN. ⎬ Oh, come on!

JEAN. ⎭ Aah!

MICK. How do you know all the old anti-British ones, Jean?

JEAN. Oh, I dunno, just pick 'em up. 'Ey – come on, don't try and get out of it.

LEN. Aye, come on, mate.

MICK. I'll give you an anti-British one.

JEAN. Yeah.

MICK. No offence . . ?

LEN. No, we can tek it, we can tek it. A good song's a good song, mate.

MICK (*sings*).

> 'Many years have rolled by
> Since the Irish Rebellion,
> When the guns of Britannia,
> They loudly did speak;
> When the bold I.R.A.
> Battled, shoulder to shoulder,
> And the blood from their bodies
> Flowed down Sackville Stree'.
>
> The forecourts of Dublin
> The English bombarded,
> Our spirit of freedom
> They tried hard to quell.

But amidst all the din
Came a voice, "No surrender!"
'Twas the voice of James Connolly,
The Irish rebel.

He went to his death
Like a true Son of Ireland,
The firing party
He bravely did face.
When the order rang out,
"Present Arms And Fire!",
James Connolly fell into
A ready-made grave.'

MICK *takes* DAWN*'s hand.*

'God's curse on you, England,
You cruel-hearted monster,
Your deeds, they would shame
All the devils in Hell.
There are no flowers blooming,
But the shamrock is growing
On the grave of James Connolly,
The Irish rebel.'

And that's all you're gettin' off me.

LEN *claps.*

JEAN. Ooh, it was good, that, Mick.

LEN. Good song, mate, good song.

JEAN. Come on, you do one now, Dawn.

DAWN. Ooh, no!

LEN. Come on, Dawn.

MICK. No, come on.

DAWN. No.

LEN. Your turn now.

DAWN. I don't know no songs.

JEAN. 'Course you do.

DAWN (*suddenly, sings*). 'This is Number One,
    And the Party's just begun,

Roll me over,
Lay me down,
And do it again.'

ALL (*singing*). 'Roll me over
In the clover,
Roll me over,
Lay me down
And do it again!'

DAWN (*solo*). 'This is Number Two,
And the party's nearly through,
Roll me over,
Lay me down,
And do it again.'

ALL *sing chorus*.

DAWN (*solo*). 'This is Number Three,
And 'e's got me
On 'is knee –'

MICK *tickles* DAWN.

'Ey! (*Laughs.*)
'Roll me over,
Lay me down,
And do it again.'

ALL *sing chorus.*

DAWN *(solo)*. 'This is Number Four
And 'e's got me
On the floor . . .'

MICK *picks* DAWN *up, and holds her down at floor level.*

'Ey! 'E's got me on the floor!
'Roll me over,
Lay me down,
And do it again.'

ALL *sing chorus.*

DAWN (*solo*). 'This is Number Five,
And 'e's mekkin'
A dirty dive . . .'

MICK *makes a dirty dive.*

'Roll me over,
Lay me down
And do it again.'

ALL *sing chorus.*

DAWN (*solo*). 'This is Number Six,
And 'e's got me in a fix,
Roll me over,
Lay me down – '

Blackout: total *darkness . . .*

MICK.   Oh.

LEN.   Ooh.

JEAN.   Blimey!

DAWN.   'Oo done that?

LEN. Oh, dear.

JEAN. It's the meter.

LEN. Oh.

DAWN. Oh, the meter's gone!

LEN. The meter's run out!

JEAN. I've got some 10p's 'ere somewhere.

LEN. Oh, dear.

MICK. Now's my chance to make my dirty dive.

DAWN *screams.*

LEN. Ey, oi!

DAWN. Sorry, Len.

LEN. Mind me.

DAWN. Did I land on ya?

LEN. No, it's alright, Dawn.

DAWN. I'm sorry.

LEN. No, you're alright.

JEAN. Blimey, I can't find 'em.

MICK. What is it you're looking for, Jean?

JEAN. I got some 10p's, I got me purse, 'ere somewhere.

MICK. Come 'ere, come 'ere, I have a handful of them here, look.

JEAN. I can't see your 'and.

LEN. It's alright, Jean, 'ere y'are, 'ere y'are, 'ang on.

LEN strikes his lighter.

JEAN. Oh, that's it; lovely. Thanks.

MICK. Got what you want?

JEAN goes to the kitchen.

JEAN. Yeah.

LEN. 'Ang on, Jean, I'll bring you a light.

The lighter goes out.

JEAN. I can't see a blind thing.

The darkness continues: MICK *assaults* DAWN. DAWN *screams. The lighter comes on again, by the meter.*

LEN. Can you see, Jean?

JEAN. Yeah, that's it.

DAWN. Stop it, Mick!

LEN. I'll put a couple more in, Jean, anyway.

JEAN. Well, that should be alright for a bit, Len.

LEN. No, we don't want it to 'appen again, do we?

JEAN. No.

DAWN. 'Ey, 'Ey, stop it . . . Jean, 'ere y'are, 'ave these.

JEAN. Len says 'e's putting some in.

DAWN. 'Be silly - 'ave them!

JEAN. Wait a minute, I'll 'ave a look, see if I've got any . . .

JEAN looks in her purse.

Look, I'll give you some 5p's for them, alright.

MICK. Put your money away, Jean, put your money away.

JEAN. Are you sure?

MICK. I am.

JEAN. Aye, alright. I'll put these on the telly. Thanks very much. You ain't robbing yourself, are you, Len?

The light comes on again.

LEN. No, no, Jean. I've just put a couple in. Keep us going for a while longer, anyway.

MICK. I dunno, I wasn't doing too bad in the dark, like.

DAWN. 'Ey – 'ey. Stop it! Dirty . . . I'm goin' on the toilet again.

JEAN. Alright.

DAWN (*going out*). Goes right through you, alco-hol.

JEAN. Once you start, you can't stop, can you?

LEN. You can't, can you?

LEN *lights a cigarette.* MICK *takes a swig from* DAWN*'s bottle of vodka.*

Pause.

JEAN. I can't drink vodka.

MICK. No, 'tis horrible.

Pause.

MICK. Not a bad old session, all the same.

LEN. No, no.

JEAN. Yeah. I like a singsong.

LEN. I do.

MICK. If you can't have a laugh and a drink on a Friday night, when can you?

JEAN. ⎫ Mmm.

LEN. ⎭ Aye, that's right, mate.

MICK. A Saturday night!

JEAN *laughs.*

LEN. Aye, Aye.

DAWN (*off*). Jean!

JEAN *gets up, and goes to the door.*

JEAN. What?

DAWN. Bring us some lavvy paper, will ya?

 JEAN *finds a toilet roll in the kitchen.*

JEAN. Oh, cor blimey, it's run out again.

LEN. She get caught short?

JEAN (*going*). Yeah.

MICK. Having a quick Eartha Kitt.

 Pause.

 Very hard on the paper, our Dawn.

 Pause.

 LEN *laughs.*

 Pause.

 The following heard off, though hardly audible . . .

JEAN. Open the door.

DAWN. Oh, ta Jean.

JEAN. You can leave that in there.

DAWN. Ah, right, ta . . .

 LEN *continues to laugh – he is considerably amused.*

MICK. Uh?

LEN (*still much amused*). Remember we used to say, 'Getting Up
 The Crack O' Dawn'?

 MICK *is not amused.* LEN's *laughter dies away.*

MICK. Jesus Fuckin' Christ, man!

LEN. Oh, sorry, Mick.

 Pause.

 Sorry, mate.

MICK. Don't let her hear you saying that, she'd chew the fuckin'
 bollocks off you.

LEN. You're right, mate, aye.

JEAN returns.

MICK. Everything alright, Jean?

JEAN. Ooh, ah. Just stuck me 'ead outside the back door. Get a bit of fresh air. Think I feel worse now. 'T in' 'alf goin' cold out. (*She lights a cigarette.*) D'you know, I'm always putting toilet rolls in that toilet; I can't be bothered tekkin' one in wi' me, and bringing it back out again, I think that's a bit petty, don't you? So everybody just uses mine.

MICK. What are they like, the neighbours, alright?

JEAN. Yeah, well . . . well I never see 'em. 'Im next door 'e works at the Europa 'Otel, 'e's never in, 'im.

MICK. 'Tis just as well for him. He wouldn't have got much sleep with us tonight.

DAWN returns, and sits on MICK's lap again.

MICK. Alright, pet?

Pause.

DAWN. 'Ey, Mick, better watch the time, you know.

MICK. Eh, we're alright for a while yet. What did you say to Theresa?

DAWN. I told 'er we'd be late.

MICK. Ah, well, there y'are, you see, we're alright.

JEAN. Yeah, 't in' often you 'ave a night out, is it?

MICK. This is it, Jean.

DAWN. I feel sick, I do.

MICK. D' you wanna go out again?

DAWN. No. I'm pissed, you know.

DAWN goes to the bed.

MICK. We're all pissed.

DAWN. Gonna get me 'ead down, Jean.

MICK. Oh, no! Wait a minute, you. Jean, if she goes to sleep, you'll not get into bed tonight at all.

DAWN. No.

MICK. Hear when I'm talkin' to you – (*He gives her a light smack.*)

DAWN. You!

MICK. Don't go to sleep.

DAWN. I won't.

JEAN. Perhaps you ought to get a taxi.

MICK. Ah 'tis not worth it, Jean, all the distance.

JEAN. No.

MICK. Jes', I don't think you'd get one this time of the night, anyway.

DAWN. Oh, go on, gerra taxi.

MICK. I will in my bollocks. (*He gives her a prod.*)

DAWN. 'Ey, Mick.

MICK. You're walking home – don't go to sleep now, I'm in no condition to carry anyone.

Pause.

JEAN. What d'you think you'll be doing this weekend, Len?

LEN. I don't know – I thought I might go to the pictures. Daresay I'll 'ave a drink.

MICK. I suppose I'll have a couple of drinks meself this weekend.

Pause.

I'll be in my usual ole place, Len, tomorrow, if you feel like dropping in for a pint.

LEN. Oh right, right. Might see you there, then, Mick.

MICK. You know . . .

LEN. Aye.

Pause.

MICK. I haven't been to the pictures this year.

JEAN. No, nor me. D' you want a cup of coffee, Dawn?

MICK. You put your finger on it, there, Jean, now that's the very thing she needs.

DAWN. Eh?

JEAN. Cup of coffee.

DAWN. Ooh, ah.

JEAN. Yeah . . .

DAWN. I'll mek it, Jean.

> JEAN *holds out an empty cup to* DAWN.

JEAN. Alright then.

> *Pause. Then they all laugh.*

JEAN. Tell you what, when you've 'ad this coffee, you'll feel better then. You'll be able to start again, won't you?

DAWN. Yeah.

MICK. You will in my bollocks.

JEAN. 'Ey, there's plenty of stuff on 'ere, you know – just 'elp yourselves.

> JEAN *goes into the kitchen.*

LEN. Oh, aye.

MICK. I have an old jar sitting there somewhere, Len.

LEN. Oh, aye . . .

MICK. Would you ever throw it over to me, like?

LEN. 'Ere y'are, mate.

MICK. Thanks very much.

LEN. There's some in there.

> *Pause.*

DAWN. What 'appened to you, Len?

LEN. Eh?

DAWN. Eh? What 'appened to you?

LEN. What d'you mean, like?

DAWN. When you went away, never come back?

MICK. Ar, for Jes' sake.

LEN. Oh, oh.

DAWN. Why d'you disappear that Christmas? We didn't know where you was. Did we upset ya? Did we? Eh? Was yer upset?

MICK. Ar, go to sleep will you?

LEN. Ar, no, no . . . what it was, I went up 'ome that Christmas, and there was a job going, so I took it – You've got to go where the jobs are, 'aven't you?

MICK. You got to go where the work is, Len.

LEN. Aye.

MICK. He was probably a bit homesick and all – you were a bit homesick, Len?

LEN. Agh, long time ago, mate: can't remember.

MICK. I know what it's like. I'd work at home if I could, but there's nothing there – I'd be sitting on my arse all day.

DAWN. Country boys, ent ya?

MICK. Country boys at heart.

LEN. Aye; aye.

DAWN. You two.

JEAN. I couldn't live in the country, me.

MICK. 'T's not everyone's cup o' tea, Jean. There's fuck all in it. I couldn't get out of it quick enough.

JEAN. Be too quiet for me.

LEN. No – best place.

JEAN. Yeah, you like it, don't you Len?

LEN. I do, I do.

DAWN. We missed you, though, Len. Didn't we, Mick? Jean?

MICK. He doesn't need me to tell him that.

DAWN. Jean: didn't we miss 'im?

JEAN. Ooh, ah, yeah, listen, d'you think you ought to 'ave this coffee black?

MICK. Aw, black is right.

DAWN. No. No, Jean.

JEAN. Are you sure?

DAWN. Ooh ah.

JEAN. Alright, then, I got a drop of milk.

DAWN. Spot of milk, Jean.

LEN. Are you working tomorrow, then, Jean?

JEAN. Oh yeah, Len, I work every Sat'day now.

LEN. 'Ope you 'aven't got an early start?

JEAN. Well, I've got to be up at seven, 'cos me shift's eight till four, see?

MICK. Aw, Jes' Christ, that's early enough for you.

LEN. It is, it is.

JEAN. Oh, it's alright, I don't mind, I can do it dead easy, 'cos I don't need a lot of sleep, see?

LEN. 'Ow d'you find working there again, then, Jean, after all this time?

JEAN. Well, it ain't the same, Len. 'Cos, you know, it's gone self-service up there now.

LEN. Aye.

JEAN. And you know, they give us these instructions, we're not allowed to touch the pumps.

LEN. Mm.

JEAN. I mean, it's ludicrous, really, when you consider the number of garages I've worked in. Still, never mind – it's 'andy to run to work if ever I 'ave to.

LEN. Aye.

JEAN. I'll just come by 'ere.

LEN. Sorry, Jean – 'ere you go.

JEAN (handing DAWN a coffee): 'Ere y'are. T's 'ot.

MICK. There ye are, Missus.

DAWN. Ooh, ah. Lovely.

JEAN. D'you wanna sit there a bit, Len?

LEN. No, no, I'm alright there, Jean, don't worry about me.

JEAN. No, I wish you would, really, 'cos I'm gettin' a bit 'ot by that.

LEN. Are you sure?

JEAN. Yeah.

LEN. Right-o, say the word if you want to come back, like.

JEAN (*getting out a cigarette*). No, you're alright. Oh, you've got one on?

LEN. Aye. Thank you.

  JEAN *takes off her cardigan.*

JEAN. Ooh, ah, I used to love it on them pumps, you know. Specially in the summer. We used to get the chairs out on the forecourt, do a bit of sunbathing.

LEN. Ah.

JEAN. I loved it. I used to be black, I 'ad.

LEN. Ha.

JEAN. We used to go out and get a cuppa tea, or a paper, and bring it back with yer, if you're a bit slack, like, you know.

LEN. Aye.

JEAN. Or sometimes we'd go out, we'd get 'alf a melon, bottle of beer, anything . . .

LEN. Ah.

JEAN. But of course it's a different job altogether now. I'm just stuck there be'ind the till, see? 'Cos I liked it when you could get out a bit, and you could 'ave a chat to people while you're filling them up with petrol.

LEN. Uh?

JEAN. But now, they just come in, they give me the money, I give 'em the change, and that's it.

LEN. Ar.

JEAN. And you know, when they modernised this, up 'ere, they twisted it all round, y'know – the pumps are on the side now.

LEN. 'Course they are, that's right.

JEAN. Yeah, whereas they were on the front before. So I've got me back to the 'Igh Road, I just stare at a bloody brick wall all day. Still, ne' mind – pays the rent, dunnit?

Short pause.

LEN. Is it that same couple running it, then?

JEAN. What couple?

LEN. That couple as ran it when you used to work there.

JEAN. There was only the Manager, Sid.

LEN. Aye. An' 'is wife.

JEAN. 'Is wife d'ain't work there.

LEN. Din't she?

JEAN. No. There was only me, Sid and Dolly.

LEN. Dolly, Dolly.

JEAN. Dolly weren't 'is wife.

LEN. Wa'n't she?

JEAN. No. You're getting confused 'cos Dolly was at Sid's Leaving Party that we went to, d'you remember?

LEN. Oh aye.

JEAN. Yeah.

LEN. Wa'n't she 'is wife?

JEAN. No.

LEN. Oh.

Pause.

'Oo's running it now, then?

DAWN (*half asleep*). Pakis, Len. Pakis running it.

LEN. Are they?

DAWN. Yeah.

JEAN. Yeah.

LEN. Treat you alright, do they?

JEAN. Yeah, why?

LEN. Lucky.

JEAN. Am I?

DAWN. Don't trust 'em, I don't.

LEN. Gettin' in everywhere now, aren't they? They want to go back where they came from.

JEAN. We'd all be in a sorry state then, wouldn't we? The 'ospitals 'd shut down, the buses'd come off –

LEN. Solve the unemployment problem, wouldn't it?

JEAN. Ah, but they do a lot of jobs that white people wouldn't touch.

MICK. Ah, now you've put your finger on it, Jean: that's right enough.

LEN. I s'pose there's something in that, aye.

DAWN. Bleedin' bus condustress yesterday, Jean's big, black piece 'er was; 'ad the babby wi'me, push-chair, bags; I said to 'er, "Scuse me, will yer ding the bell for me please, because I wanna geroff at Willesden Lane.' Did 'er fuck ding the bell, Jean. Nearly ended up in bleedin' Cricklewood, I did. Give 'er a mouthful. Told 'er where to geroff. Jungle.

JEAN. It in't 'cos 'er's black; I mean, I know a lot of white bus condustresses'd do that to you.

DAWN. No . . . they'm lazy buggers, they am.

MICK. Ah, no. Fair do's, now. I've worked with them, on the sites – like yourself, Len. Some of them are very hard workers. Big fuckin' bastards, an' all.

LEN. Oh, the West Indians are alright.

MICK. Ah, yeah – 'tis the fucking Scotchies I can't stick.

JEAN. Oh, well, we're all the same underneath, in't we?

LEN. Ar, but the thing about the Pakis is, they don't try to change their ways – they don't try to fit in.

JEAN. Would you try an' fit in with them, if you went over there?

LEN. Aye.

JEAN. Would ya?

LEN. Aye.

JEAN. You'd eat all the same food, curries an' all that, you'd live in the same conditions?

LEN. No.

JEAN. Oh, you're saying you wouldn't fit in?

LEN. I wouldn't live like them.

JEAN. But you expect them to live like you when they come over 'ere?

LEN. Aye – that's different, int it?

JEAN. Oh, is it? What's different about it?

LEN. Well, 'oo'd want to live the way they live?

JEAN. D'you know 'ow they live?

LEN. Aye.

JEAN. Ow?

LEN. Well . . .

JEAN. Eh?

LEN. Well . . . you know . . .

JEAN. Yeah, I know – I just wondered if you knew.

Long pause.

MICK. I had a curry the other night. I don't know how they take it. Went right through me. I could've shat through the eye of a needle.

Pause.

Funny the way you never see a Pak in a pub, like.

JEAN. Well, that's 'cos some of them are Moslems, see, an' er, it's against their religion to drink.

MICK. Oh, I get it.

JEAN (*gets out cigarettes*): One o'these, Dawn? Oh, look at 'er – 'er's gone, in 'er?

DAWN *is asleep.*

MICK. She's away with the band.

JEAN. Len?

LEN. Can you spare it?

JEAN. Yeah.

LEN. Oh. Don't mind if I do, Jean, thank you.

He lights JEAN's *cigarette.*

'Ere y'are.

Pause.

JEAN. 'Ave you been anywhere nice, Len, in the car, since you've been down 'ere?

LEN. Oh, no.

MICK. D'you know what, Jean?

JEAN. Mm?

MICK. This man has offered to take the kiddies for a run in the jamjar.

JEAN. Oh, ah, they'll love that, Len.

MICK. They'll love that.

LEN. Take 'em off your 'ands, like.

MICK. You've the heart of a lion, boy. They're a terrible handful.

JEAN. Where you going to tek 'em, Len?

LEN. Oh, thought I might go to the zoo, like.

JEAN. Oh, ah, they'll love that, won't they, going to the zoo?

MICK. They'll love that.

JEAN. Not so long back, you know, I took 'em to a funfair. 'Course, they wanted to go on everything, so I 'ad to go on everything with 'em – I was terrified, me.

MICK. They're a terrible shower of gangsters. They hunt in packs.

MICK *goes out.*

Pause. DAWN *is still asleep.*

JEAN. Ooh, ah, they'll love that, Len, going out in the car.

Pause.

LEN. Well – better start thinking about going.

JEAN. What sort of car you got?

LEN. Cortina.

JEAN. Oh, ah, they're nice, en' they?

LEN. Aye, it's a bit old, this'n, it's still a runner, like.

Pause.

JEAN. Good job you ain't driving tonight.

LEN. Aye, huh.

Pause.

JEAN. Well, you'll 'ave to come down the garage, get some petrol
off me.

LEN. Aye, I will, huh.

Pause.

JEAN. 'Er's going to 'ave an 'ead on 'er tomorrow, en 'er?

LEN *laughs.*

JEAN. D'you wan' a cup o' coffee, Len?

LEN. No. No, I'll be off in a minute, Jean.

JEAN. You can stop if you want.

Very long pause.

MICK *returns, whistling quietly to himself. He tests a couple of cans,
then goes over to* DAWN, *and smacks her bottom.*

DAWN. Ow. Don't.

MICK. Come on, Missus, time to go time.

DAWN. Silly.

DAWN *goes back to sleep.*

MICK *returns to examine the beer cans at the table.*

MICK. There's a drop left in here, Len: d'you want some?

LEN. Oh, aye, finish it off, like.

MICK. What about you, Jean?

JEAN. No, I'm alright.

MICK. Are you sure?

JEAN. Mm.

MICK. Oh, Jes', you look a bit tired, girl. I'll tell you what, I'll get this woman shifted, and then you can have a lie down to yourself.

(MICK *touches* DAWN's *stockinged foot. She jumps, and bangs her head on the headboard*).

DAWN. Ooh, blimey, Mick!

MICK. What's wrong with you?

DAWN. Made me bump my bleedin' 'ead, you did.

MICK. Egh, you're alright!

DAWN. Ooh.

MICK. Come on!

DAWN. 'Ey!

MICK. Come on, it's time to get up.

DAWN. Don't be rough with me!

MICK. Well, we have to go, like.

DAWN. I know – I'm ready, en' I?

MICK. Alright, then.

DAWN. Silly. (*She lies down again.*)

MICK. Two minutes. I'll give you two minutes. (MICK *returns to the table, and the drinks.*) Are you walking up the road, Len?

Pause.

Uh?

DAWN *gets up.*

DAWN. I'm tired.

MICK. Are you sick?

DAWN. No. (*She goes out, to the loo.*)

MICK. Yeah – well, don't be all night.

Pause. LEN *and* JEAN *say nothing and do nothing.* MICK *faces the drinks, and sings the following in a relaxed, intermittent kind of way, and drinks a bit.*

MICK (*sings*). 'Hairy eggs and bacon,
  Hairy eggs and ham!
  Hairy eggs and bacon,
  Hairy eggs and ham!
  Hairy eggs and bacon,
  Hairy eggs and ham!
  Hairy eggs and bacon,
  Hairy eggs and ham!'

  DAWN *comes back.*

DAWN. Come on Mick, chop-chop.

MICK. I'll just knock this back.

DAWN. 'Er'll be wondering where we am, Theresa. Eh? Ooh, blimey, Jean, you'll 'ave us 'ere all bleedin' night at this rate. Where's my shoes? Ooh ah, I've gorrem: no – there they am. (*She puts on her shoes.*)

MICK. Uh, we did a bit of damage here tonight.

LEN. Aye.

DAWN. I want no rows with Theresa, Mick.

MICK. Ach.

DAWN. Funny bugger, 'er, you know. Couldn't be doin' with it, I couldn't. (*Quietly, to* JEAN.) Alright, am yer, Jean?

JEAN. Yeah, yeah.

DAWN. Alright am yer, Len?

LEN. Aye.

DAWN. Yeah – lovely to see ya.

LEN. Aye – nice to see you, Dawn.

MICK. Now here, Missus, don't be making yourself comfortable.

DAWN. 'Course I ain't.

MICK. Ar, you're not putting on make-up this time of night?

DAWN. Got to walk up the 'Igh Road, en I?

MICK. Who the fuck'll be looking at you?

DAWN. Heh, you don't know, do you? Only a bit o' lippy, any road.

MICK. You're all lip. Jean.

JEAN. Mm?

MICK. Very nice.

JEAN. Yeah.

MICK. Thanks very much. Grand old session.

JEAN. Yeah.

MICK. Ha? Bit of an old singsong.

JEAN. Yeah.

MICK. Aw, lovely.

JEAN. Yeah.

MICK *rubs the back of* JEAN's *head*.

MICK. We won't let it be so long again.

JEAN. No.

DAWN. Come round next week, Jean.

JEAN. Yeah, I will.

DAWN. Lovely night, Jean.

JEAN. Yeah.

DAWN. Lovely. Enjoyed yourself?

JEAN. Yeah, I 'ave.

DAWN. 'Course you 'ave. Want to get out more often, you do, Jean, you know – you do – 't en't good, stoppin' in, ooh no. Enjoyed myself, any road. Lovely! Enjoyed myself! Know where we live, Len!

(The following dialogue runs simultaneously with the preceding passage, and begins after: 'Yeah, I will.')

MICK. Len: put it there, baby. No fuckin' problems.

LEN. No.

MICK. Okay?

LEN. Right-o, mate.

MICK. I'll be at my usual old station tomorrow.

LEN. Right-o.

MICK. If you feel like dropping in for a pint.

LEN. Right.

MICK. If I don't see you tomorrow, I'll see you through the week.

LEN. Okay, mate, right. Right.

DAWN (*concluding*). Know where we live, Len!

LEN. Aye.

MICK. Thanks for the ole soup, Jean.

JEAN. Yeah.

DAWN. Don't forget to come round, Jean.

JEAN. Yeah, I will next week.

DAWN. Babbies am askin' for you, you know.

MICK. Oh, Dawn –

DAWN. Eh?

MICK. D'you remember the old Baby Bellings?

DAWN. Ooh, blimey. Don't.

MICK. We had one of them in Messina.

DAWN. We did.

MICK. D'you remember that Christmas?

DAWN. Ooh, ah! Twenty-nine pound turkey 'e brought 'ome, Len, six pound 'o sausages.

MICK. You see, the way it was, Len, I got caught up in the pub on Christmas Eve, and by the time I got to the butcher, the only thing he had left was about the size of a pig. Lord Jesus, you could've stuffed the turkey with the Baby Belling.

DAWN. I nearly killed 'im, I did, Len. You 'ad to break in upstairs.

MICK. We did an' all; I put my shoulder to the door of the flat upstairs; the fellow was away for Christmas, like, you know.

DAWN. You remember that, Jean, you was there, I was out 'ere with Tracy.

JEAN. Yeah.

MICK. She was there. 'Twas a very nice bird, anyway.

DAWN. Lovely bird.

MICK. Come on, Missus.

DAWN. Ooh – we'm goin'.

MICK. Time to go – you got to carry me home now!

DAWN. Ooh ah!

MICK. See that, Len? I get carried home.

LEN. Oh, aye. Aye.

MICK. Jean: very nice. Thanks very much. No fuckin' problems.

LEN. Tara then. Tara Dawn.

DAWN. See you. See you, Jean.

JEAN. Tara.

MICK. I'll see you, Len.

LEN. Tara mate, all the best like.

MICK. Ooh, for Jesus' sake.

DAWN. Ooh, blimey, Mick – I can't carry you.

MICK. Aw, go on – ah?

DAWN. Do me flippin' back in, you.

MICK. Oh Jesus Christ. Jes', tis dark.

DAWN. Ooh blimey! Ah.

MICK. Put that light on there, will you?

DAWN. Aye. 'Ey, don't forget to open this door quiet, now.

MICK. Okay.

DAWN. Shut it quiet 'cos you'll wake the 'ouse up.

MICK. Alright, no fuckin' problems. Jes', 'tis fuckin' chilly.

DAWN Ooh ah.

MICK. Come here.

DAWN. Yeah.

> MICK *and* DAWN *have faded away down the street.*
>
> *Silence: a long pause. Then . . .*

LEN. Surprised to see you again.

JEAN. Yeah. Surprise to you, an' all.

> LEN *laughs.*
>
> *Pause.*

LEN. They don't change, them two, do they?

JEAN. No – no, they don't.

> *Pause.*

LEN (*belches*). Oh – I beg your pardon, Jean.

JEAN (*gets out cigarettes*). One of these, Len?

LEN. Oh, I don't mind if I do, Jean, thank you. 'Ere y'are.

> LEN *lights* JEAN*'s cigarette.*
>
> *Pause.*

LEN (*getting up*). Look, Jean, I think I ought to go really – y'know
. . .

JEAN. Oh no, you don't 'ave to.

LEN. No, you've got to get up early in the morning.

JEAN. Oh well, that don't matter.

> *Pause.*

LEN. You don't want me to stay.

JEAN. Yes, yes I do. I mean, 'ave another drink if you want.

LEN. No, I've got, I've got some 'ere.

JEAN. Well, 'ave a top-up then, or summat.

LEN. No, I've 'ad enough to drink.

JEAN. Yeah, well . . . praps we all 'ave, eh?

LEN. Aye.

Pause.

LEN. She's a character, is Dawn, isn't she?

JEAN. Yeah. Yeah, 'er is. 'S been a good friend to me, 'er 'as.

LEN. Aye.

JEAN starts to cry, quietly, and with her head down.

What's up?

LEN gets up, and puts his cup down.

Eh?

He puts his arm round JEAN, and takes it away almost immediately.

What's the matter?

JEAN. Just pleased to see you, that's all.

LEN Oh! (*Laughing.*) Eh?

He hugs her.

Ah! Eh? That's better. Nothing to cry about.

He stands up. JEAN starts to cry again at the same time. LEN bends down again to put his arm round her, gets a bit stuck, and stands up. He puts out his cigarette, and he takes her cigarette, and puts that out. Then he crouches down, and hugs JEAN.

LEN. We've all 'ad a lot to drink tonight, that's all.

JEAN (*crying*). But I drink all the time.

JEAN cries throughout the following, never raising her head from her lap. And somewhere during this speech, LEN starts to cry, too.

I just sit 'ere. I didn't enjoy meself tonight. Didn't want to talk about anything, just got upset. There was . . . there was a bloke 'ere earlier . . . an' em . . . Dawn was 'ere, an', uh . . . 'is wife came, an' that's 'ow the bed broke . . . I don't even like 'im. I don't tell 'er anything.

Pause.

I 'ate living 'ere. She thinks I don't go out with anybody. An'
I do. Well, I never like 'em. They don't like me, they just like
'itting me.

Pause.

I've been pregnant.

Pause.

I've always 'ad to get rid of 'em on me own.

Pause.

When she was 'avin' 'ers, I was 'aving mine. I lie to 'er all the
time. I just want to die.

LEN *is still crying, and hugging* JEAN. *He stands up suddenly.*

LEN. Me leg's gone to sleep.

JEAN. I'm 'ot.

LEN. Shall I put the fire off?

JEAN. No.

LEN. D'you want a cup of coffee?

JEAN. No. Just didn't think.

LEN. Eh?

JEAN. I was big-'eaded.

LEN. What about?

JEAN. I was always 'orrible to you.

JEAN *moves to the bed, and lies on it, continuing to keep her face
away from* LEN.

LEN. Eh?

JEAN. You were nice to me and, em . . . I just wanted to 'ave a
good time . . . stupid.

Pause.

LEN *crouches down by her, and hugs her for a few moments. Then he
separates.*

LEN. You ought to go to bed.

JEAN. No point in going to bed now. I'll just sleep 'ere.

LEN. D'you want me to go?

Pause.

JEAN. 'Don't mind.

LEN. I'll stay if you want.

Pause.

You go to bed – I'll sleep in the chair.

JEAN. You'll 'ave to 'ave a blanket.

LEN. I'll be alright.

JEAN. It goes cold in the night.

LEN. I'll be alright.

Pause.

I've got me coat. Come on.

JEAN sits up.

JEAN. In' it a mess in 'ere?

LEN. Aye. (*He puts his coat on the armchair, and takes off his jacket.*) I'll just go to the toilet.

JEAN. Will you put the big light off? Just there.

LEN. Oh, aye.

LEN goes out. JEAN throws a cushion and the counterpane from her bed onto the armchair. Then she undresses. LEN returns at a moment when she happens to be naked from the waist upward. Neither of them are at all bothered by this: each takes the other's presence in these circumstances for granted. LEN picks up the counterpane.

LEN. Will it be alright if I 'ave this?

JEAN. Yeah. Yeah.

LEN takes off his shoes. JEAN gets into bed. LEN prepares the armchair.

JEAN. You can leave that fire on, 'cos it'll go off when the meter runs out.

LEN. Shall I put that light out?

JEAN. Yeah.

LEN *goes towards the bedside lamp. He sits on* JEAN's *bed.*

Pause.

LEN. You alright?

JEAN. Yeah.

LEN. Good night.

He kisses her, gently and briefly. Then he puts out the light, and finds his way back to the chair, lit by the electric fire. He settles in the chair, gathering the counterpane and coat round him.

Long pause.

Slow fade to blackout.

The End

Songs

DANNY BOY

I KNEW A FARMER

I knew a far-mer, and I knew 'im well. I knew 'is daugh-ter and 'er name was Nell. She was so pret-ty and on-ly six-teen, And I showed 'er the works of my thresh-ing mach-ine. (f)

CHORUS

I 'ad 'er, I 'ad 'er, I 'ad 'er, I 'ay. I 'ad 'er, I 'ad 'er, I showed 'er the way. They were the best days of my life, I would say, And I spent them a-lead-ing young mai-dens a-stray.

IT'S THE SAME THE WHOLE WORLD OVER

It's the same the whole world o — ver, It's the poor what gets the blame, It's the rich what gets the plea — sure, Ain't it all a bloom-ing shame?

WHEN I WAS YOUNG, I USED TO BE

when I was young, I used to be as fine a lad as ev-er you'd see, and the Prince o' Wales, he said to me, "Come and join The Brit-ish Ar-my

CHORUS

Too-ra-loo-ra-loo-ra-loo, They're look-ing for mon-kies Up in the zoo, And if I had a face like you, I'd join the Brit-ish Ar-my.

MANY YEARS HAVE ROLLED BY SINCE THE IRISH REBELLION

ROLL ME OVER

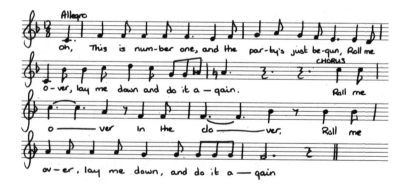

HAIRY EGGS AND BACON

Moderato

Hair-y eggs and bac-on, Hair-y eggs and ham!

Hair-y eggs and bac-on, Hair-y eggs and ham!

Hair-y eggs and bac-on, Hair-y eggs and ham!

Hair-y eggs and bac-on, Hair-y eggs and ham!